THE GREAT IRISH TENOR
John McCormack

THE GREAT IRISH TENOR

John McCormack

GORDON T LEDBETTER

TOWN HOUSE
DUBLIN

First published in 2003 by

TownHouse, Dublin
THCH Ltd
Trinity House
Charleston Road
Ranelagh
Dublin 6
Ireland

This text is based on an earlier work by the same author,
The Great Irish Tenor (Duckworth & Co., 1977).

Plate captions
page 18: Portrait of McCormack taken around the time
of his Metropolitan Opera debut.
page 96: McCormack in the role of Rodolfo in Puccini's *La Bohème*.
page 220: McCormack broadcasting for NBC.
page 241: McCormack on the set of *Song O' My Heart*.

1 2 3 4 5 6 7 8 9 10

A CIP catalogue record for this book is available from the British Library.

ISBN: 1-86059-178-7

Cover design by Anú Design, Tara
Text design and typeset by Anú Design, Tara
Printed by CPI Bath

Contents

For My Mother

Acknowledgements

Any biography depends upon the help and generosity of many people. David Bateman started the ball rolling in the first place by suggesting the book and better still providing me with an introduction to Treasa Coady of TownHouse, and to both I am very grateful.

I would like to thank in particular Eddie O'Connor for lending me records and memorabilia and for many kindnesses. For much encouragement and for directing me to various sources, I owe a debt of thanks to Dr Richard T Soper; and to the McCormack scholar John Ward, for generously providing me with information and visual material from his own researches, and I acknowledge with thanks permission from the him and the editor of *The Record Collector* to quote from John Ward's article 'McCormack on Brighton Pier'. I have made use of Paul Worth's fine website on the tenor and I am grateful to him for permission to quote from a McCormack letter to Bishop Michael J Curley. My thanks to Peter F Dolan for correspondence and I acknowledge with much thanks his authoritative article, 'John McCormack, Mastersinger: A Short Account of his American Career' in *The Sword of Light* (Spring 1974) as source material. To Gearoid O'Brien, author of *McCormack & Athlone,* I owe much thanks for sharing his expert views with me and for permission to quote from his work. Padraic O'Hara kindly gave me permission to quote from *Letters of a Legendary Singer.* To Una Breen, for the opportunity to photograph material in her possession, I am most grateful, likewise to Dave Fitzgerald for allowing me to photograph the labels of his very rare John O'Reilly discs. My thanks to Seamus Kearns for making his collection of memorabilia available to me, and to Elizabeth Augureau, for taking the time and trouble to visit the Théâtre Champs Élysées and for carrying out newspaper research in Paris. Bea McManamon kindly provided information on the tenor's holiday at Shean Lodge in County Mayo. Thanks are also due to the staff of the newspaper library in Colindale London; the Music Library at the Ilac Centre, Dublin; and the staff at the library of Trinity College

Dublin, and I acknowledge the generous help provided by Bríd Conneelly; also Mary Trotter; and to the New York Public Library and the Library of Congress. I would also like to express my thanks for the help provided in various ways by: Dr Gabrielle Langdon; Patrick Viale; Susan Maxwell; Patrick P Clarke; Ita Hackett; Elizabeth O'Brien; Ray McSharry; Dr Jack Flanagan; Rosemary ffolliott; Maciej Smolenski; Gary Owens; Hilde Eiselen; Annette Mende-Hand; Diane O Ota; Retha Cilliers; Wallace Beatty; Adrian and John Beatty; Andrew Glenn-Craigie; Brian Fawcett-Johnson and Gráinne Thomas.

I acknowledge with thanks permission from the late Cyril, Count McCormack and the Library of Congress for the use of letters from John McCormack to his manager, Charles L Wagner.

To Carol Ann McCormack I am most grateful for her illuminating conversations and for use of memorabilia.

I acknowledge also with gratitude material from the National Library of Ireland, the archives of the Royal Opera House, Covent Garden; the Metropolitan Opera, and the Teatro alla Scala. I am grateful for material from the John McCormack Society; from the late Liam Breen and Robert L Webster. I remember with gratitude conversations with the late Perceval Graves who knew McCormack in his early London days and whose papers I have drawn upon. I acknowledge the use of Miles Kreuger's article 'A Hollywood Venture' on the film *Song O' My Heart*. The cartoon by Jimmy Hatlo is reprinted with special permission of King Features Syndicate.

I take this opportunity to acknowledge with thanks permission from W H Allen & Co. for permission to quote from Lily McCormack's *I Hear You Calling Me*; to Curtis Brown Ltd for a quotation from Bing Crosby's *Call Me Lucky*, published by F Muller Ltd; also John Farquharson Ltd for permission to quote from Henry Pleasants' *The Great Singers from the dawn of Opera to our Own Time* published by V Gollancz Ltd. I am grateful too to G P Putnam's Sons for material from C L Wagner's *Seeing Stars* and for *Two Centuries of Opera at Covent Garden* by Harold Rosenthal; Alfred A Knopf for *The Story of the Metropolitan Opera 1883–1950* by Irving Kolodin; Charles Scribner's Sons for *Too Strong for Fantasy* by Marcia Davenport. Cassell & Co for *All That I Have Met* by Mrs Claude Beddington; The MacMillan Co. for *A Quaker Singer's Recollections* by David Bispham; University of Oklahoma Press for *Oscar Hammerstein's Manhattan Opera House* by John Frederick Cone; Doubleday & Co. for *Great Singers on Great Singing* by Jerome Hines; The Old Athlone Society for *John McCormack and Athlone* by Gearoid O'Brien; Small, Maynard & Co. for *Singer's Pilgrimage* by Blanche Marchesi; Cambridge University Press for *The Cambridge Companion to Singing* edited by John Potter; Doubleday & Co. for *Going My Way* by Bing Crosby; Duckworth & Co. for *The Record of Singing* by Michael Scott; Faber and Faber for John Hetherington's *Melba*; Hamish Hamilton for *Am I Too Loud?* and *Farewell Recital* both by Gerald Moore, and for *A Voice in Time* by Jerrold Northrop Moore; The Victor Talking Machine Co. for *The Victor Book of the Opera*; Little, Brown & Company for *Requiem for a Yellow Brick Brewery* by John Briggs; Boethius Press for *Monte Carlo Opera 1910–1951* by Dr T J Walsh; Yale University Press for *Opera in America, a cultural history* by John Dizikes; Oxford University Press for *Toothpicks and Logos, Design in Everyday Life* by John Heskett. I acknowledge with thanks material quoted, as well as visual material, from: Grove's *Dictionary of Music and Musicians*; *The Times*; the *Daily Telegraph*; *The New York Times*; *The New York Herald*; *The Sun*; *The Philadephia North American*; *The Boston Sunday Post*; *The Japan Times*; *The Freeman's Journal*; *The Melbourne Herald*; *Gramophone Magazine*; *Hi-Fidelity* magazine; *Journal de Monaco*; *Il Mattino*; *The Irish Times*; the *Irish Independent*; the *Irish Press*; *The Freeman's Journal*; *The Daily Herald*; *The Dundalk Examiner*; *Punch*; *The Tatler*; *The Illustrated London News* and *The Graphic*.

The author and publisher have endeavoured to contact all copyright holders. If any errors have inadvertently been made, corrections will be made in future editions.

Most writers owe a debt greater than is generally acknowledged to their editors and I most grateful for the painstaking work of Marie Heaney, Claire Rourke and Deirdre O'Neill.

To my sister, Audrey Baker, I am, as always, grateful for reading the manuscript and for making many suggestions.

Gordon T Ledbetter
August 2003

Introduction

The generation who heard McCormack in the flesh is now gone. How well I remember the eagerness with which old timers would recall the awe and enchantment they felt at the beauty of his voice and the power of his personality. Time moves on. I now find myself sandwiched between that generation and the rising one in which the question might be asked, 'Who was *he*?'

He was without question, the greatest singer Ireland has ever produced. Not only for the beauty of the voice but for his musicianship, his power over language. He demonstrated that in all kinds of music. Whatever he sang, he sang with complete idiomatic security. It was as if his overwhelming desire to communicate enabled him always to get to the heart of things. And he always got to the heart of his listeners, giving the illusion, even in large auditoriums, of person-to-person intimacy. He was much more than an entertainer. For he articulated, brought to the surface, the innermost hopes and longings and sentiments of those who heard him; an embodiment of his times. And his Irishness, his boyish charm (how often that description was used) won hearts wherever he went.

Nothing can equal a live performance. Nevertheless, McCormack's art was one that largely transcended the limitations of sound recording. The immediacy of his communication, the economy of means by which he achieved it and a good measure of the beauty and the purity of the voice are apparent on records. Even those made close to one hundred years ago during the acoustic age of recording, before the microphone entered the studio in 1925, retain these qualities. Records were not cheap in the early days of sound recording, and many a less than well-heeled collector had to make difficult choices. McCormack 78s were cherished in countless homes, kept almost s family heirlooms.

It is curious how often people will tell you the very first time they heard a McCormack record and which one it was. As likely as not, they will quote lines from the song in question; melody and language were as two sides of the same coin in McCormack's art.

It is remarkable how one never seemed to be compromised for the benefit of the other. I can remember the first time I heard him, on radio, when I was still a child. It was during a family holiday in Kerry and Radio Éireann, as it was then, played the Herbert Hughes arrangement of 'The Star of the County Down'. The impression has remained with me ever since. An uncle with whom I went to live had an exciting collection of 78s, McCormack among them, into which he allowed me to delve. These old shellac discs went hand in hand with the romance surrounding the old wind-up gramophone, the smell of oil, the cranking of the handle, the simple miracle of sound coming directly from a groove in a round plate, without the intervention of electricity. And the musty, heady smell of records! To be sure, modern transcriptions on LPs and CDs especially provide cleaner reproduction and the availability of records from the past has never been greater, but on an impressionable youth, these old records and the method of playing them carried the sense of summoning up an enchanted past.

The records were one thing. In addition, my uncle had heard McCormack and not a few of his contemporaries and had a fund of anecdotes. He would often recall the tenor's rapport with an audience and two of the greatest sopranos with whom McCormack sang. He remembered the enduring thrill of Melba singing Tosti's 'Goodbye' at her farewell in Dublin in 1926; and receiving a red rose from her after the concert was another precious memory (the rose has long since turned to dust but he programme has survived). Another was meeting Tetrazzini at the Theatre Royal in 1933. She liked the attentions of a young man who had the temerity to knock on the door of her box, my uncle recalled, and she whipped out of her bag a photograph (dated 1908!) and signed it. It can be found in this book.

There were other old timers who I had the great good fortune to meet, who shared their golden memories with me: an old school friend of McCormack's still living in Athlone; avidly listening to anecdotes from the McCormack family; trips to Kings Langley in Hertfordshire to talk with Perceval Graves who shared digs with McCormack and attended his Covent Garden debut; the thrill of going to Philadelphia to meet the critic Max de Schauensee, who had heard nearly all the 'great ones', Caruso included, ten or twelve times, and wrote with special affection on McCormack. So, too, did the author Henry Pleasants whose perceptions and thoughts on singing, which he shared with me, meant more to me than he could ever have known. Through them, I was drawn into a golden world of great singers, who seemed united in a vividness of performance and lyricism that belonged to an age that is gone.

The odyssey of travelling back in time through recorded sound is an intoxicating pleasure. There are few pleasures like it and, listen to whom you will, the conclusion is hard to resist: McCormack was, vocally, the *beau ideal* of the lyric tenor.

This is his story and the story of his times.

Gordon T Ledbetter

CHAPTER ONE

An Uncertain Start

In the early years of the 20th century, the two most celebrated tenors in the world were Enrico Caruso and John McCormack. A century later, they are still regarded as two of the greatest singers ever recorded. Caruso was McCormack's senior by only eleven years and, unusually for rival singers, the two were good friends.

A story about the two tenors became part of New York folklore: McCormack emerging from his hotel, spotted Caruso on opposite side of the street and called across to him, 'And how is the world's greatest tenor?' To which Caruso replied, 'John, since when have you become a baritone?' The story indicates the esteem in which McCormack was held by the Italian, who, by general consensus, was the operatic colossus of his time.

McCormack's greatest achievements were made in a different sphere: in the concert hall as a recitalist he had no rival. In terms of vocal endowment, the two tenors had little in common, what they did share was an immediacy of communication that could draw a response from a much-wider public than the habitual opera and concertgoer.

'A singer of the people,' remarked the American critic Max de Schauensee in a pen portrait of McCormack, while also describing him as a 'singer's singer'. As such, McCormack could lay claim to being the finest musician among singers of his time. All this was achieved with little formal training – McCormack was never near an academy or a university. Perhaps if he had been, he would not have reached the hearts of millions in the way that he did.

Above: The River Shannon and bridge at Athlone around 1900. The woollen mills are to the left of the Georgian building beside the bridge. *Left:* Andrew and Hannah McCormack, the tenor's parents.

McCormack's origins were less than promising. He was born in Athlone in the Irish midlands on 14th June 1884. The town had grown up around the 12th-century Anglo-Norman castle on the edge of the River Shannon, where the native Irish had withstood the onslaught of William of Orange's forces during 1690–91. Its strategic position at the Shannon crossing where east meets west – County Westmeath on the east bank, County Roscommon on the west – had made Athlone a British garrison town, a feature that may have contributed to the nationalist sympathies that were to cause McCormack

Above: This plaque was unveiled by Dr Vincent O'Brien, the tenor's first teacher, on 17th July 1938. Right: The house on The Bawn where John McCormack was born.

problems later in his life. At the time of McCormack's birth, Athlone was bucking the national trend of emigration and had a population of about 7,000. It was prospering through the local woollen mills, work which brought McCormack's father to the town from Scotland.

In fact both the tenor's parents were Scottish, as was his paternal grandmother. His grandfather, Peter McCormack, is described in the 1871 census in Scotland as a forty-eight-year-old labourer from Ireland (in fact he came from Sligo), with a wife, Isabella, two years his senior who was born in Dalmellington, East Ayrshire. By 1871, they had a family of four children – two sons and two daughters. Andrew, the second son, was then eighteen and described as a tweed finisher and he remained in the woollen business all his working life. In 1874, Andrew married Hannah Watson, a power-loom weaver of Presbyterian stock, from Ladhope in the county of Selkirk in the Scottish borders, who became a Roman Catholic on her marriage.

Andrew made the journey from Scotland, going first to Lisburn, County Antrim, from where he made the move to Athlone and took up work in the local woollen mills as a labourer, eventually becoming a foreman. He and Hannah had a family of eleven children, six of whom survived into adulthood. John Francis was the fourth child, born in the family house in a narrow street called The Bawn (off Mardyke Street) in that part of Athlone that is east of the Shannon in County Westmeath. The house is still there, with its single door and window on the ground floor and two windows above. By the time of the 1901 census, the household had moved to 5 Goldsmith Terrace, which had five rooms and three front windows. Andrew, now forty-five years old, is recorded in the census as a tweed finisher and as being able to read and write; Hannah, aged forty-four, was only able to read. By 1911, when there are only the parents and a son, James, living at home, they have an eight-roomed house at 4 Auburn Terrace, again with three windows in front; and Hannah, now married for thirty-six years, is recorded as being able to both read and write.

Andrew seems to have been a gruff sort of individual. The tenor summed up his relationship with his father in a remark made in an interview for the American magazine, *Musical Leader*, in 1917: 'My father told me I would never amount to anything in the world.' A short phrase that says a lot. In his head, McCormack did not doubt his accomplishments; emotionally he may not have found it so easy. He was competitive all his life, always liked to win an argument and was never slow to start one. His gifts as a communicator amounted almost to a compulsion, as if, as it has been suggested, each time he had to prove his worth. It would explain how his art, even when his voice was failing, remained urgent, immediate and fresh. His relationship with his father might also explain why McCormack was always his own man and would never bow to authority if he thought it misplaced.

Andrew had a tenor voice and legend has it that it was a better one than his son's. This seems unlikely, as there is hardly another tenor on record who had McCormack's purity of tone, seamless and effortless throughout the vocal range; but certainly Andrew was fond of singing and this may well have influenced his son. Dr Vincent O'Brien, McCormack's first voice teacher, recalled that he 'was often heard to remark that "his father's fine tenor voice, given favourable conditions of wind and weather, could be heard in action, on 'Flow gently, Sweet Afton' or 'The Bonnie Banks of Loch Lomond' as far away as the famous bridge itself".' Perhaps there was an element of rivalry between father and son. Certainly the tenor was to show something of that himself later in life. His son, Cyril, would recall, without perhaps seeing the irony of it, that when, as a child, he was asked to do his party piece in front of visitors, his father could never keep silent. 'Now I'll show you how it should be done,' he would say, and proceed to do exactly that.

The house in Athlone had no piano but McCormack said he could never remember a day at home when there was no singing. It seems singing was in the family blood, spontaneous and unschooled. Athlone had no opera house and McCormack would have had little exposure to so-called classical music during his childhood. But making music of some sort is better than not making music at all and, even as a youngster, McCormack showed that 'he had something in the voice'. A school colleague, even as an old man, could recall the sound of McCormack's voice in the school choir, admitting that he was drawn to evensong simply to hear him.

McCormack first attended school when his father took him up on his shoulders

Above & right: Marist Brothers' school photograph taken in the early 1890s. John McCormack is the third pupil on the left in the row below the teacher in the bowler hat. *Far right:* Group photograph of pupils at Summerhill College, 1900. McCormack is on the extreme left in the centre row, with a light cap on his knee.

and brought him down to the local Marist Brothers where he was enrolled on 1st July 1889. The school had been established just five years earlier. Education in Athlone improved throughout the 1880s, with illiteracy rates being halved in the twenty years to 1890. The young McCormack was able to make the best of his educational opportunities. He proved a quick and eager scholar and excelled in languages and mathematics. From the Marist Brothers, he moved to St Mary's Male National School, enrolling on 14th October 1891. He was regarded as a bright pupil and took his first music lessons from Brother Eimard McNamara. In 1896, at the age of twelve, he won a scholarship to the Diocesan College of the Immaculate Conception

23

The earliest-surviving programme of a concert featuring the tenor. It was given at the Father Mathew Hall, Athlone, on Monday, 28th December 1903 and was conducted by Vincent O'Brien. He was assisted by six other performers, none of whom came to prominence. McCormack sang Adams' 'The Holy City' in the first half of the programme and Crouch's 'Kathleen Mavourneen' in the second, before teaming up with James Ryan in Benedict's rousing duet 'The Moon Hath Raised'.

Father Mathew Hall,
ATHLONE.

Programme of

Mr. J. F. McCormack's

Concert ....

Monday, December 28th, 1903.

Conductor:
Mr. VINCENT O'BRIEN, I.C.M.

Doors open at 7-30 p.m.
Commence at 8-0 o'clock sharp.
Carriages, 10-30 o'clock.

ATHLONE PRINTING WORKS

of Summerhill (now Sligo College) in County Sligo and maintained himself there with further scholarships.

Perhaps the most commonly quoted anecdote about McCormack relates to a school concert held at Summerhill College. A school maid came up to him after it, praised his singing but regretted that he had sung in a foreign language. He had, in fact, sung in English. The criticism, he later said, spurred him to improve his diction, which he did with such success that it is sometimes said that his diction was his greatest virtue. It was, indeed, one of them. There have been other singers with exemplary diction, but to concentrate solely on this accomplishment is largely to miss the point. It was not diction in itself that set McCormack apart, but his ability to converse on a musical line, to tell a story in song, as it was so often said, to point up language without compromising the musical line.

While still in his teens, McCormack was involved with the Gaelic League and often sang at gatherings around the country. It was at this time that he was known for performing rousing rebel songs such as 'The West's Awake' and 'When Shall the Day Break in Erin?'. Also, at this time, he sang a number of times in the Father

Mathew Hall in Athlone. One such concert, held in January 1903 in aid of the Athlone Female Technical School, brought this prescient review from an anonymous critic, who may have been a local choirmaster, Michael Kilkelly, who had taken an interest in the young lad:

> In sweetness and fullness of tone his singing of 'Avourneen' was certainly one of the finest items that could be heard at a provincial concert or perhaps at a city concert hall. It is safe to say that if Mr McCormack went in for professional singing he would meet with much success.

In one concert, held at the Father Mathew Hall, having sung 'The Snowy-Breasted Pearl' and 'When Other Lips', there were encores for him to sing 'The West's Awake'. This presented a conflict of interest. There were a number of British army officers and their wives in the audience and, in deference to them, McCormack refused to sing the song. This brought down upon his head the charge that he was pro-British. In those days, sentiments of being for or against the Union tended to loom large in people's thoughts, and the fact that McCormack's father Andrew was from Scotland, a blow-in and one who had risen through the ranks in the Woollen Mills, may also have created tensions between some of the townspeople and McCormack.

Like many another Irish lad brought up in a Roman Catholic household in those days, McCormack had given thought to joining the priesthood. He remained strong in his faith throughout his life but, by the time he left Summerhill College in 1902 aged eighteen, his thoughts had already turned to a career in singing. Predictably, this did not meet with much sympathy from his father. There were insufficient funds for a university course so, under parental pressure, McCormack sat the scholarship examination for entry into the Dublin College of Science. There were only twenty places available in that year and McCormack came twenty-first – much to his father's disgust. His father then insisted that he enter the civil service and McCormack got a job as a clerk in the postal service. But friends in Athlone, Michael Kilkelly among them, regarded this as a waste of talent and wrote to Dr (then Mr) Vincent O'Brien (1871–1948), conductor of the Palestrina Choir of the Pro-Cathedral in Dublin. As a result of these approaches, O'Brien auditioned McCormack and offered him a place in the choir. This was McCormack's chance and he took it, despite his father's mis-givings – and he remained a singer for the rest of his life. The job in the postal serv-ice had lasted about a fortnight.

Vincent O'Brien was a well-rounded musician, experienced in choral work and the training of young voices. He introduced his new chorister to tonic sol-fa and began his grounding in musical theory and sight-reading. Gerald Moore, the English

*The tenor wearing
his Gold Medal
from the Feis.*

Cover of the Feis Ceoil Syllabus of Prize Competitions held between 18th and 23rd May 1903. Note the price of 1d.

pianist who accompanied the tenor during his latter years, commented that McCormack was one of the two best sight-readers of music he had known. Given that Moore had played for virtually all the great singers of his time, this was praise indeed. (The other singer he had in mind, incidentally, was the German baritone Dietrich Fischer-Dieskau.)

Most aspiring young musicians in Ireland enter the Feis Ceoil, the national musical festival or competition held annually in Dublin, which is open to both amateurs and professionals. O'Brien coached and coaxed McCormack for the tenor section in the Feis of 1903. He was a reluctant debutant at this stage of his life, shy and uncertain. He was also short of funds and did not have the price of the entry fee, which had to be paid for him. A worse problem, however, and one he suffered from all his life, was nerves before a concert. But, once he was on stage and singing, his nervousness would fall away as he engaged with the music and his audience. And so it was to prove at the Feis.

Each contestant was required to sing the same two pieces and then read 'an easy piece at sight'. The two songs selected for the tenor section were 'Tell Fair Irene' from Handel's *Atalanta* and the Irish air 'The Snowy-Breasted Pearl'. The adjudicator was Signor Luigi Denza (1846–1922), professor of singing at the Royal Academy of Music in London (better remembered now for his song 'Funiculì, funiculà') and the accompanist was Hamilton Harty (1879–1941), who was soon to make a reputation for himself as a composer. The order of appearance of the fourteen competitors was by ballot – McCormack was the last to sing and, at nineteen, the youngest. Whether from panic or good judgement, when Harty struck up the opening bars to 'Tell Fair Irene', McCormack immediately stopped him, saying it was far too fast. Harty started again and, when McCormack had got through, there was a spontaneous outburst of applause from the audience – remarkable, as it was against Feis protocol to applaud at all. Signor Denza, rising to his feet, turned to the audience and said, 'You have yourselves chosen the winner', and McCormack was awarded the Gold Medal. He was on his way.

Confusion exists as to when Lily Foley, shortly to become McCormack's fiancée, entered the Feis. The first biography of the tenor, *John McCormack: His Own Life Story* by Pierre Key, contains McCormack's recollection of his Feis success:

> I profited; and another profited, a young soprano, Miss Lily Foley, whom I had never met. Miss Foley had surpassed her rivals with astonishing ease… As I listened to her, at the Feis, I thought to myself, 'I'd like to sing with her.' And in the fall of that same year I had my wish.

Lily herself in her biography of the singer, *I Hear You Calling Me*, noted: 'I'd just won a Gold Medal myself for a solo in Gaelic and was so pleased with myself I didn't go to the tenor competition and so missed John McCormack.' In fact, it was the previous year, 1902, that Lily Foley had won the Gold Medal in the soprano section for solo singing in Irish. Her real name was Elizabeth but she was always known as Lily and she was also a pupil of Vincent O'Brien.

The Palestrina Choir photographed on a visit to St Patrick's Cathedral, Armagh, in 1904. The twenty-year old McCormack is fourth from the left in the back row. Dr Vincent O'Brien is second from the right, front row. Edward Martyn (1859–1923), founder of the choir and, with W B Yeats and Lady Gregory, of the Irish Literary Theatre (later the Abbey Theatre) is in the back row, sixth from the right, in a dark suit and glasses.

John and Lily's paths had crossed at local concerts without them ever having been formally introduced and when Lily observed John on his way to early mass at the Pro-Cathedral and he, turning round, caught her looking at him, they felt a mutual attraction. Nothing much came of that until they were both engaged to sing in Athlone in 1903 as supporting artists to the noted Dublin baritone William Ludwig (1847–1923) – who had forsaken his family name of Ledwich for Ludwig, because of its continental cachet. Lily had sung for Ludwig before, and had arranged to travel down with him and his two daughters on the train. As she tells the story in *I Hear You Calling Me*:

> ...at the last minute before the train left John arrived at the Broadstone Station, looking pale and sickly. Forlornly he announced that he had a bad cold and couldn't sing, but that he would come along to show that he was willing. Mr Ludwig said, 'What you need, young man, is someone to look after you. And here is the very little lady. Miss Foley, may I introduce John McCormack?'
>
> We both blushed furiously and John never spoke a word on the trip. But he did sing at the concert and had an ovation. Then the doctor ordered him to bed for a week's rest, so I didn't 'look after' him on the return journey! I have often wondered if Mr Ludwig ever recalled his prophetic words in the years to come.

So began a relationship that was to be lifelong. *I Hear You Calling Me*, in addition to outlining McCormack's international career, is an affectionate, indeed loving, portrait of a marriage that, against the odds in a profession notorious for its instability, stood the test of time.

James Joyce was another aspiring tenor and pupil of Vincent O'Brien who competed in the Feis in 1904, the year after McCormack. Joyce had been in the audience when McCormack had won the Gold Medal and was inspired to enter the Feis himself. Gold eluded Joyce as he refused to attempt the sight-reading exercise and was awarded the Bronze Medal instead. It is said that he threw his medal into the River Liffey in disgust. Joyce's singing ambitions faded with time, but he retained an interest in singing throughout his life. He closely followed McCormack's career as well as that of the Irish *tenore robusto* John O'Sullivan (1878–1948), whose career in Paris Joyce took it upon himself to champion. McCormack and Joyce appeared at least once in the same concert at the Antient Concert Rooms, Great Brunswick Street, now Pearse Street, on 27th August 1904. They both received warm reviews. 'Mr James A Joyce,' reported *The Evening Telegraph* on 29th August, 'the possessor of a sweet tenor voice, sang charmingly "The Sally Gardens", and gave a pathetic rendering of "The Croppy Boy".' The paper went on to declare that:

> Mr J F McCormack was the hero of the evening. It was announced as his last public appearance in Ireland [before going to London], and the evident feeling of the audience at the parting, seemed to unnerve him a good deal. His voice is one of great resonance, as well as of high range, and his powerful notes were heard in a varied selection of Irish melodies. The audience seemed as if it would never see enough of him, and twice he had to respond to triple encores, while he was recalled times almost without number.

Newspaper advertisement for a 'Grand Irish Concert' to be held in the Antient Concert Rooms, Great Brunswick Street (now Pearse Street) on 27th August 1904, the one occasion in which McCormack and James Joyce appeared on the same programme.

Stereo photograph of the Irish village at the St Louis World Fair. Behind the bandstand is a mock-up of Blarney Castle.

Clearly, even as a youngster of twenty, McCormack had begun to make a reputation for himself.

McCormack and Joyce were not to meet again until the 1920s by which time, of course, their paths had diverged widely. Joyce, however, had kept up with McCormack's career and both McCormack and Athlone featured in *Finnegans Wake*. The tenor became the model for Shaun the Post, of whose voice Joyce wrote:

> …and cert no purer puer palestrine e'er chanted panagelical mid the
> clouds of Tu es Petrus, not Michaeleen Kelly, not Mara O'Mario…

The 'puer palestrine' refers, of course, to the period McCormack spent with the Palestrina Choir and no one ever chanted with greater purity 'panagelical' or 'Panis Angelicus', the setting by César Franck to words by Thomas Aquinas. This hymn was closely identified with McCormack's career and he sang it at the Eucharistic Congress held in Dublin in 1932. The singing of the Palestrina boy chorister was not surpassed by Michaeleen Kelly – Michael Kelly (1762–1826) – remembered for his amusing if not wholly reliable *Reminiscences* and for singing two roles, that of Don Basilio and Don Curzio in the first production of Mozart's *Le Nozze di Figaro* in Vienna in 1786. 'Mara O'Mario' is a conflation of two names, the Limerick-born tenor Joseph O'Mara (1866–1927) and the aristocratic Italian tenor Giovanni Matteo, Cavaliere di Candia (1810–1883), better known simply as Mario, probably the most celebrated tenor of the mid-19th century.

This is all high praise indeed, but Joyce could have heard only one of three tenors whom he compared with McCormack, namely Joseph O'Mara whose career spanned the turn of the century. Like McCormack, O'Mara was trained in Milan and the two tenors appeared together in concert at least once, at the Theatre Royal, Dublin, in November 1906. That is about as far as a comparison could go. O'Mara was noted for his exciting acting style and had a bright, clarion, dramatic voice while McCormack was never a dramatic tenor. Michael Kelly received mixed reviews during his career, one critic saying his voice 'is dreadfully wanting in sweetness' whereas McCormack was noted for just that quality. As regards the third tenor, Joyce was only two years old when the great Mario died. Someone who was familiar with both Mario's voice and McCormack's was Mario's own daughter, Mrs Godfrey Pearse, and she drew a comparison between the beauty of tone of both singers. The comparison suggests McCormack, in his effortless vocal production, was more of a throwback to the singing style of the 19th century than a precursor to that of the 20th or 21st centuries.

As a result of their success in the Feis, both McCormack and Lily Foley were invited to cross the Atlantic to appear at the St Louis World Fair in 1904. McCormack would sing his repertoire of Irish ballads in English and Lily, presented as 'Ireland's exponent of Gaelic Song', would sing in Irish.

McCormack himself had no Irish worth speaking of, as it had not been spoken at home or taught at school. He was to sing in five languages: English, French, German, Italian and Latin but not Irish, despite, ironically, being regarded as the quintessential 'Irish tenor'. But, of course, had it not been for the fact that English was his natural tongue, it is unlikely his popularity in the States and elsewhere would have reached the heights it did. Lily at one point tried to teach him some Irish and early on he did attempt 'Úna Bán' in the original, but he never felt at ease with the language and retained the song in his repertoire only in translation.

Lily's parents thought she was too young for the trip to St Louis and relented only when it was agreed that she should have a chaperone, in the event her older sister Molly. Although primarily a trade fair, visitors to the Irish village, with its mock-up of Blarney Castle, were provided with musical entertainment. McCormack soon had reservations, as Lily was to recall:

> Everything was going well enough with the Irish Village until the management decided to add a comic Irish turn with a 'stage Irishman' to liven up the programme. We all protested… Before any decision was reached John, with his quick temper, handed in his resignation, which was accepted just as promptly. I think they found John a rather difficult young man to handle… This impulsiveness of John's remained to the end.

Lily Foley's carte-de-visite photograph taken in St Louis. She is described as 'Ireland's exponent of Gaelic Song'. She appears to be wearing an engagement ring.

Miss Lily Foley
IRELAND'S EXPONENT OF GAELIC SONG
IRISH INDUSTRIAL EXHIBITION
Worlds Fair St. Louis, 1904
Murillo Studio, 1314 Olive St., St. Louis

This stand against stage Irishness might appear as exceptionally high-minded and courageous for a young man just leaving his teens. But there was another side to the issue. As Lily added, John, having gone out to the St Louis World Fair, realised that 'he was only losing time at work of this sort and he longed to get on with serious study'.

Serious study, he now realised, meant going to Italy and he had set his heart on studying with Maestro Vincenzo Sabatini in Milan to whom he had an introduction. So McCormack returned home from St Louis intent on raising the necessary funds to support himself. It would be a mere five years before he returned to the United States when his impact would be immediate and triumphant.

However, there was one problem that needed resolving before leaving St Louis. As Lily tells it, John left it to the last moment:

> On John's last day at the Fair we were going upstairs to the restaurant in the Irish Village and met Molly coming down. John said, suddenly, 'Let's give her a surprise. Let's tell her we're engaged.' I said, 'Let's,' thinking what a shock it would be to her but also feeling in my heart that I'd like it to be true. John said with a beaming smile, 'Congratulate us, Molly. Lily and I are engaged.' Molly merely shrugged her shoulders and said, 'Don't talk such nonsense at your age! You've got to think of your future first.'

There was more of this sensible talk from the older sister until she was satisfied John had taken in everything she had said. When she had gone, John turned to Lily and said, 'Lily, let's make it true. Let's *really* be engaged. I won't have an easy moment unless you promise not to look at another boy, *I* promise *you* I won't look at another girl.' We may wonder if the chronology here is correct as Lily appears to be wearing an engagement ring when she was photographed for her *carte-de-visite* photograph in St Louis, an event that presumably occurred shortly after her arrival in the town. One way or another, Lily's sister may have been party to the engagement, but when Lily returned to Dublin in November, at the end of her contract, she did not dare reveal the happy event to her parents.

The immediate challenge that faced McCormack was how to raise funds to get to Italy. Whatever about the quality of his voice, he did not cut much of a figure in those early days. Lily described him as 'frail', something of an undernourished urchin, quite a contrast to the robust figure he was to present in just a few years' time. The late Mrs Josie Hoyle heard him at this time and found him gauche, describing him to the author as 'standing like a ploughboy', his arms held firmly down by his sides. But he was prepared to learn. McCormack acknowledged that it

Left to right: Box labels on early cylinder recordings; Note the proprietor's name John F Coyne, cycle engineer, of 115 Upper Dorset Street and the hand written – and misspelt – name of the singer. As the sale of bicycles was seasonal, the sale of records were intended to boost business during the off-season months. It was some time before recordings had their own specialised retail outlets. Lid label for Edison cylinder of 'Love Thee Dearest', 1904. The dealer's name appears to have been roughly cut off the label, possibly because the cylinder passed to another dealer. This, and the fact that the tenor's name is missing its 'Mc', shows the rough and ready ways of the young recording industry.

was the actress Constance Collier who taught him how to present himself on stage. To his friend Mrs Claude Beddington he confessed, 'Twas Constance first took me in hand for stage-deportment. When I was a young fella I used to come on to the concert-platform like this' – here he lumbered across the room like a bear walking on its hind legs – 'but she taught me to hold me spine straight and me head up, and I've been grateful to her ever since.' Gauche he may have been, but the voice invariably attracted attention, not only the quality of it, but the communicative gift that went with it.

Benefit concerts were one way of raising money. A committee was formed in Athlone, the Father Mathew Hall was booked and local performers were called upon to participate in order to keep costs down. Nationally, some £200 were raised by benefit concerts and other means, yet of this a mere £30 was raised in Athlone. A letter, dated 19th July 1905, from McCormack to Michael Kilkelly expressed bitter disappointment:

> …it is evident the Concert was a dire failure and after expressing my deep gratitude to you and the committee I can only say what is my firm conviction, that some influence was at work against me and I have an idea of the quarter it came from and it is hard lines when in a strange city a man will be supported and in his very birthplace he will be injured by petty spites and jealousies.

35

John O'Reilly Zonophone labels – different name, same singer.

Vincent O'Brien, as well as Lily's father and others, organised a benefit for him in Dublin and well-wishers came from as far afield as Athlone to support him. But McCormack retained an ambivalent attitude to Athlone thereafter.

A windfall came through the making of a series of recordings, not for one recording company, or even two, but for three separate companies all operating in London. This would be inconceivable today; not only that a singer should move between several recording companies but that so young a man should be engaged at all. McCormack was just twenty when he made his recording debut and he was to continue to record regularly right until the end of his active career and, indeed, for some years after his official retirement. His discography thus encompasses a span that is unlikely to be repeated by any other singer.

At the turn of the century, the recording industry (which had been greeted at first as a toy and a scientific novelty) had been operating commercially for about a decade. Recordings were being made in two ways: as wax cylinders, roughly the size of the cardboard insert of a toilet roll, which whirred around at about 160 rpm; and flat plates or discs, made of shellac, that revolved at anything from the low 70s or lower to 90 rpm or more. To hear a singer in the same key as he was recorded, it was necessary, of course, to play the recording back at the same speed. A discrepancy of three revolutions for a disc recorded at 78 rpm would result in the drop or rise of about a semi-tone. Indeed the term '78' is a misnomer for there was no agreed speed standard. Where transpositions took place, as was common in the studio when a singer had a compliant accompanist, the key (unless indicated on the label, which it rarely was) and the speed at which the disc should be played, were matters of conjecture – and, to this day, playing speeds are still debated for many early historic recordings. Little wonder that the celebrities of the opera world were not inclined to take the recording industry seriously and were to take some persuading before they committed themselves to it.

In the milieu of the time, recording was open to newcomers and to all sorts of musicians who would not get a look-in once the industry was well established. Nor did copyright mean what it does today. Many a music-hall singer or banjo player made money from recording his repertoire first with one company, then another, sometimes using a pseudonym, sometimes not. McCormack did just the same, styling himself first of all as Mr J F McCormack or John McCormack.

Only in 1974, in an article by John Ward, Alan Kelly and John Perkins entitled 'The Search for John O'Reilly' in *The Record Collector*, was what had long been suspected confirmed: that a number of records made by McCormack had been issued under a pseudonym. The researchers established that several matrix numbers from among unpublished recordings listed in McCormack's recording sessions for the Gramaphone & Typewriter Co. had, in fact, been issued by its sister company, Zonophone, but under the name of Mr John O'Reilly. These discs are extremely rare, but there is no question that John O'Reilly and John McCormack were one and the same person. The only alternative: that another singer had interpolated recordings during McCormack's sessions, is not credible. How did the name John O'Reilly come about? We can only speculate. It has been suggested that McCormack took the name of Father John O'Reilly, a friend of the time. Perhaps, as John Ward has surmised, McCormack took engagements in music halls in London around this time and preferred to present himself under a pseudonym. This would have made sense; when it came to auditioning for opera he would not have wanted what little reputation he had as a singer to be associated with the music hall.

The very first records McCormack made were a series of two-minute black wax cylinders of ballads for the Edison National Phonograph Company on Gray's Inn Road, in September 1904. Russell Hunting, an actor turned recording entrepreneur and prolific recording artist himself, recalled getting a call from Jim White of Edison to say:

> Our... agent in Dublin wants us to record a chap who sings Irish songs in the real Irish manner, and wants to send him over here. He says he will sing for almost nothing but thinks we should, between us, pay him ten pounds.

> Well I agreed to pay *half*, and although I don't know exactly what White paid him, I gave him £5 for one week's work… and I have never been thanked so much by anybody… (White told me… that he sang for pennies along the *waterfront*).

If McCormack ever did sing on a waterfront, there is no other evidence to confirm it. Maybe White was making a quip for there is no doubt the young man was on his uppers. Hunting continued: '…when I first saw him… [he] was wearing a coat that had seen many better days, upon which a few pieces of fur (on which the moths had dined frequently) were sewn.'

At this session with the Edison Company, McCormack recorded ten cylinders one after another with no second or third takes. All these cylinders have a spoken introduction by the singer himself. They reveal a midlands accent somewhat flattened perhaps by his time in Dublin. Played on an original Edison 'Standard' phonograph, the singing sounds primitive, with the portamenti exaggerated and the singer scooping for the high notes. The dynamics are fulsome, but this may, at least in part, be due to the recording apparatus itself and to the singer moving injudiciously towards and away from the recording horn. In 'Molly Bawn', the fourth recording, you can clearly hear how he allows the voice to crack for emotional effect – an effect he was to repudiate a little later – like a child playing at being an Italian tenor. What modern electrical transpositions reveal is that the diction was much better in 1904 than might otherwise be apparent, and the singing sounds smoother and more controlled. McCormack's instincts were felicitous from the start. The impression he gives on these recordings is of his jaw hanging loosely as he aimed to avoid or eradicate any extraneous tension in his vocal emission. His problem was that the effect of striving for relaxed vocal emission carried over to his vowels and his articulation and, as a result, the vowels are lacklustre. He had yet to forge a vocal identity for himself.

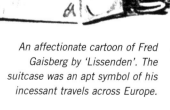

An affectionate cartoon of Fred Gaisberg by 'Lissenden'. The suitcase was an apt symbol of his incessant travels across Europe.

Photograph taken of McCormack around the time of his first visit to London. He appears to have dispensed with the moth-eaten coat.

But do these first records show anything of what was to come? It may be being wise after the event, but the whole-hearted commitment is there; and whatever about the diction, the singing appears to be led by the words rather than the words being squeezed and elongated to fit the melody. This approach would remain with McCormack all his life and had much to do with the compelling communicative artist he became. At this stage, he comes across as singing for the sheer joy of it and he engages by his youthful verve.

A week or two later, McCormack was at 21 City Road for recording sessions with the Gramophone & Typewriter Company and made the acquaintance of Fred Gaisberg, a seminal influence in the history of sound recording.

Gaisberg had come over from the States in 1898 equipped with disc-recording apparatus and another wonder of the age, a bicycle with pneumatic tyres. It was through Gaisberg's tireless efforts that many of the great Victorian singers, who almost certainly would not otherwise have done so, were persuaded to make records. Gaisberg got word of McCormack through Russell Hunting. Strange as it now seems, at that time the cylinder business and the disc business were not necessarily regarded as rivals on the assumption that the owners of phonographs would be interested only in cylinders while gramophone owners would likewise buy only discs. 'No one was keener to welcome an Irish tenor than I,' Gaisberg recalled, 'since I was alive to the commercial possibilities among the Irish Americans, who showed the most idolatrous worship of the bards.' He may have written this with the benefit of hindsight. To his cost, Gaisberg did not sign McCormack to an exclusive contract; instead he offered him twenty-five guineas, a gramophone and complimentary discs. The impression that McCormack first made on Gaisberg was less than favourable:

> He struck me as an over-grown, under-fed, unkempt youth – loosely built, pale faced, disorderly dark hair, untidy clothes, very bad teeth, and worn down shoes… and he was drinking too much… His eyes were piercing dark and he had very little to say, but that little showed him decidedly confident of himself – almost aggressive…
>
> We all took an interest in this rough diamond… We recorded the very popular Irish songs, and I recall the difficulty he had when singing Fs and Gs… I was particularly struck with this defect, and thought what a pity in so promising a voice – for the quality was truly beautiful… While making his records he revealed to me that he would shortly be leaving for Italy to study with the well-known Maestro Vincenzo Sabatini [in Milan].

It is surprising that someone as knowledgeable as Gaisberg should express disappointment in the tenor's top register, he was still, after all, hardly more than boy. The voice and the artist still had plenty of growing to do.

With the Gramophone & Typewriter Company over two consecutive days, 23rd and 24th September 1904, McCormack recorded on both seven-inch and ten-inch shellac discs, repeating everything he had done for Edison and adding another twenty or so ballads, including for the first time what was to become one of his most popular recordings 'Kathleen Mavourneen'. He made three recordings of 'Killarney' and it is one of these that, in later years, McCormack would play to friends, without identifying the singer and then ask for their opinion as to whether the singer should think of a professional career. The joke would be then revealed when the friends expressed horror at the singing. But maybe they would not have done so if they had heard 'Killarney' or indeed any of these G&Ts as modern transcriptions. The voice is clear and forward and well recorded, the singing more careful than on the Edisons, although 'Molly Bawn' still gets the emotional treatment with the voice cracking on the word 'pining', not once, but twice.

Finally, in November 1904, McCormack recorded a series of two-minute black wax

Maestro Sabatini. The maestro was immediately impressed with McCormack's natural vocal placement.

cylinders for the Edison-Bell Consolidated Phonograph Company, the same fare as before, with the addition of 'Dear Little Shamrock' and his first opera recording – 'Once would my heart with the wildest emotion' from Benedict's *The Lily of Killarney*. McCormack was never to appear in this opera, but it was the kind of thing that went down well in Edwardian drawing rooms. All in all, in less than two months, McCormack had made something in the order of fifty recordings and he was only twenty years old.

While in London for these recording sessions, up in the gallery of the Royal Opera, Covent Garden, McCormack heard for the first time the voice of Enrico Caruso. He never forgot the occasion, 'That voice rings in my ears after thirty-three years,' he was to write, 'the memory of its beauty will never die.' On a youthful impulse he got hold of a photograph of his new idol – and added an inscription to himself from Enrico Caruso. It would not be long, however, before he would have the genuine signature with a warm inscription to go with it.

With what money he had, McCormack set off for Milan early in 1905. When Sabatini first heard him, he apparently said, 'I cannot place your voice, God has done that.' The placement of the voice, the manner in which the voice is projected, is the most fundamental requirement of singing. Occasionally, a singer arrives on the scene whose placement is entirely natural, a combination of instinct coupled with an exceptionally responsive musculature. It can be seen more obviously in the felicitous movements of the 'born' dancer or tennis player for instance. In the same way, McCormack was a 'born' singer. No doubt what Sabatini worked on was stretching McCormack's voice, increasing its range and power, bringing into play those Fs and Gs that Gaisberg expressed disappointment in. Not that the mature voice ended there. His top Bs & Cs became full throated and clear, his pianissimi a hallmark of his art.

Sabatini was in his mid-seventies and kept a studio at 4 Via Victor Hugo in Milan and, at first, set his pupil to work on exercises. Teacher and pupil got on well. The maestro recognised in McCormack an assiduous worker. Sabatini's wife was English as were the elderly sisters, the Misses Beetham, with whom McCormack lodged, in Via Breva, an asset on his arrival as he had no Italian worth talking of. But he soon learnt the language, speaking it so fluently that Guglielmo Marconi used to joke that, although he had been born in Italy, McCormack spoke better Italian than he did. Italian influenced McCormack's singing in English, the vowels became more rounded and focused – occasionally too emphatically for some tastes as with the broad A vowel and the hard E vowel, heard for instance in his pronunciation of the word 'Tralee'.

He was back in Ireland for the summer of 1905 and word of his talents was getting round. It was at this time that Mrs Claude Beddington, a London society lady, heard him for the first time and could hardly believe her ears. She recalled in her memoirs *All That I Have Met*:

> While I was staying with my parents at Ballycumber, King's County [County Offaly], in the summer of 1905, my mother said to me: 'I hear the foreman of the Athlone Woollen Mills has a son with a lovely tenor voice; will you hear him sing, and then we can see what can be done for the boy?'
>
> To this I replied: 'A tenor voice off *this* bog?… Never! A boy with good hands on a horse, yes – but a singer? Don't you believe it!' However we finally arranged that the youth should come over to Ballycumber on August 12th for an audition. Now, it is manifestly impossible to judge a voice if you are accompanying it on the piano, so my mother played for him, whilst I sat at the farthest end of the room. Never shall I forget the thrill John McCormack's voice gave me that day, with its natural Italian colouring and true tenor quality.

He returned to Sabatini at the end of the summer and was back home at Christmas dividing his time between Dublin and Athlone. His heart was now set on an official engagement with Lily. His family were adamantly against it, and he was afraid to

The tenor during
his early years as
an opera singer.
He looks every
inch the Edwardian
gentleman.

McCormack in the title role of Mascagni's L'Amico Fritz in which he made his debut at the Teatro Chiabrero, Savona on 13th January 1906.

approach Lily's father, Patrick, directly. So he asked Lily's mother to intercede on his behalf. She did not want to do this, but McCormack worked her round to it. The result was an outburst of disapproval. Lily's father would not countenance such a thing, although he relented to the extent that the matter could be raised again in two years' time. This did not suit John, once he had made up his mind about something, he always wanted to go through with it. But at least he could return to Milan knowing that Lily was of the same mind as himself. 'John took a little gold ring set with three tiny diamonds which father had given me for Christmas and changed it over to my engagement finger making me promise to keep it there as much as possible… I often did some very fast switching, but so far as I know he [Lily's father] never discovered it!'

McCormack was still an immature singer when, on 13th January 1906, he made his first appearance in opera, singing the title role in Mascagni's *L'Amico Fritz* at the Teatro Chiabrero in Savona. It is perhaps surprising that Sabatini allowed his pupil to perform publicly after just a few months' tuition, but McCormack may have persuaded him of the necessity of earning money. The stage name he used was Giovanni Foli – the Italian form of his own first name and Lily's surname spelt so as to look as if it was Italian. His debut might have gone a lot worse. What he remembered of the performance was: '…being scared of the high B flat and knowing that I could not possibly be heard over what seemed to me then a very large orchestra, I just opened my mouth wide, struck a dramatic attitude but made no sound. The audience, thinking they heard a beautiful B flat, insisted on an encore.' He then took the part of Faust in Gounod's opera at the Teatro Verdi, Santa Croce sull'Arno. This time he was less fortunate. High notes cannot be evaded indefinitely. His voice did crack and he fled the stage!

In the spring of 1906, Lily's father died. McCormack returned to Ireland in late May to sing in an amateur performance of Gounod's *Faust* conducted by Vincent O'Brien, and stayed on for the summer. He approached Lily's mother again. He put it to her that either he married Lily or he would not return to Italy to continue his studies. With misgivings she gave her consent. John then took his fiancée to Athlone to meet his parents. There was singing every night around the fireside, Lily remembered, and she got on well with Andrew and Hannah until John announced their intentions.

> How the atmosphere changed! To start with, they had much to say on the subject of his foolhardiness in making singing his career: and now to think of taking on the responsibility of a wife seemed to them nothing short of madness. John didn't report any of this to me but I 'felt' it. I insisted on cutting my stay short and, before I left, John and I had a long talk. I suggested that we

45

wait for at least another year and he said, 'It's up to you, Lily. I
promise you'll never starve – are you willing to take the chance?'
I said I was.

They were married at the Pro-Cathedral in Dublin on 20th July 1906, at the early
hour of 7.30 am so that they could catch the mailboat to London the same day.
Bridget Foley and Thomas Bisette (Lily's brother-in-law) were the witnesses. John
wore his first frock coat and silk hat, Lily an 'ultra stylish blouse' with a bone
collar to her ears. Bending her head, she said, to sign the register, was a struggle.
A cartwheel hat covered in white flowers set off her trousseau. No wedding picture
survives because they tore it up by mutual consent! The highlight of their brief
honeymoon in London was visiting Covent Garden and hearing the voice of
Enrico Caruso.

In Italy, despite finding that the food did not agree with her, Lily, adaptable by
nature, soon settled in. She gives the impression that wherever her husband's career
might take him, she saw her role as supporting him. 'We were happy in our huge
bed sitting room, with a piano in one corner, where John and his operatic coach
would work for hours, while I, with my little ironing board in another corner,
pressed our clothes and kept them tidy.' Lily and John made one duet together – 'Ai
nostri monti' from *Il Trovatore,* recorded in 1906 – presumably more out of fun than
anything else. This piece is written for a contralto, providing perhaps a more congenial range for Lily if she had not been exercising her voice. When it was played
back, she claimed she was horrified with the sound of her own voice, and the disc went
the way of the wedding photograph. Lily did, however, continue to sing occasionally
at small gatherings.

The young couple had a routine in Milan. Lily would accompany John to his
daily lesson with Sabatini, half an hour's stroll from their lodgings. Spare time was
spent exploring the city, not least the art galleries, for John was developing a taste for
paintings; and they visited the opera and sat in the famous Galleria observing the
'great ones'. There were few greater than the Neapolitan tenor Fernando De Lucia
(1860–1925) whom McCormack pointed out to Lily one day. The manner in which
De Lucia bowed and shaped his phrases, redolent of a stringed instrument, made an
impression on McCormack that ran deep. Their paths were to cross a few years later
in Naples.

According to Beddington, after just a few months tuition with Sabatini, the maestro
had said: 'Giovanni, you need not stay with me any longer; all you have to do now
is to go out and make your fortune. With that voice the world is yours!' It does not
sound like the remark of a singing teacher, especially as it was directed towards an
untried country boy with a relatively small voice and no stage experience worth men-

The great Enrico Caruso striking a dramatic pose in Verdi's Ernani.

47

Originally a sports cartoonist, Jimmy Hatlo came to be associated with a long-running series of cartoons entitled 'They'll Do It Every Time', which he started in 1929. In this cartoon, from 1961, he took up the anecdote of McCormack hailing Caruso with the words, 'And how is the world's greatest tenor?' To which Caruso replied, 'John, since when have you become a baritone?'

tioning. But what is certain is that, with little vocal training, McCormack achieved a consummate vocal technique.

He was, by his own admission, poor at auditions. In Milan, his great hope came when he sang for Giulio Gatti-Casazza at the Teatro alla Scala. He again cracked a high note and lost that opportunity. As it turned out he never would sing in La Scala.

After a few further minor engagements in small opera houses in the north of Italy,

McCormack found himself without work. He had developed his voice under Sabatini but, nevertheless, failed to make much headway with his career in Italy. He was now faced with some difficult decisions. Lily was expecting their first child and money was running short. They decided to leave Italy and return to London. While in Milan, McCormack had written letters to London, looking for work. He was a good networker, not one to expect work simply to come to him. By the time he left Milan in September 1906, London must have seemed to hold more promise and had the advantage of being closer to Dublin, where Lily would have her confinement.

CHAPTER TWO

The Move to London

The young couple found lodgings at 12a Torrington Square, Bloomsbury. Perceval Graves, the son of the Irish poet Alfred Perceval Graves and a law student in London at this time, had digs in the same house and left this pen portrait:

> McCormack had a top floor bed-sitter and the use of a lovely little Bord piano on which he taught himself to play. He had a tremendous power of concentration. When I first knew McCormack he didn't give a damn how he dressed. How could he, considering that without private means he had to work for every penny he earned.
>
> We were lucky in our landlord, Jim Balmer… who was fond of good music and a popular member of the Choughs, an amateur music club, and in John's early days, when he was just able to rub along, Jim Balmer put quite a few engagements in his way.
>
> But I think he first came into his own in London when our landlord lent him five pounds to buy a fur coat and which he repaid just as soon as he could. It gave him a great sense of comfort and well being.
>
> John and I used to walk down the Strand, the singer sporting a Trilby hat, somewhat the worse for wear. He generally carried

a packet of boiled sweets in his pocket. Except for very rare occasions he was a non-smoker [later, however, he became an enthusiastic smoker].

McCormack immediately set about following up the letters he had written from Milan and making further contacts. To his disappointment, the Gramophone & Typewriter Co. wanted nothing more to do with him. So, for the moment, he confined himself to making cylinder recordings. In July 1906, he recorded half a dozen Irish ballads, four of which are rousing, patriotic songs, for the Sterling Company. For a singer trying to make his way in London, it might have been thought an unwise choice of material.

Also from this period, there are a couple of Pathé hill and dale discs (so called because the needle vibrated up and down in the groove, not from side to side, as was the technique used by most companies), which may be transcriptions from the recordings made for Russell Hunting at Sterling. There is also a single Edison four-minute black wax cylinder extant dating from December 1906 of 'Home to Athlone'.

It is said that the new manager at Edison, James White, wanted McCormack to sign an exclusive contract but McCormack refused. This is interesting in the light that he *did* sign an exclusive contract with Odeon – who manufactured discs – a short time later. Perhaps McCormack had a hunch that the future lay with discs rather than cylinders, although this was by no means clear at the time even to those working in the industry who

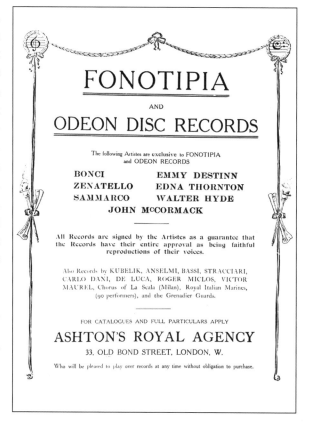

Advertisement for Fonotipia and Odeon records. Note the claim that 'All Records are signed by the Artistes as a guarantee that the Records have their entire approval as being faithful reproductions of their voices'. Some of the greatest names recorded for Fonotipia and Odeon.

FONOTIPIA

AND

ODEON DISC RECORDS

The following Artistes are exclusive to FONOTIPIA and ODEON RECORDS

BONCI	EMMY DESTINN
ZENATELLO	EDNA THORNTON
SAMMARCO	WALTER HYDE
JOHN McCORMACK	

All Records are signed by the Artistes as a guarantee that the Records have their entire approval as being faithful reproductions of their voices.

Also Records by KUBELIK, ANSELMI, BASSI, STRACCIARI, CARLO DANI, DE LUCA, ROGER MICLOS, VICTOR MAUREL, Chorus of La Scala (Milan), Royal Italian Marines, (90 performers), and the Grenadier Guards.

FOR CATALOGUES AND FULL PARTICULARS APPLY

ASHTON'S ROYAL AGENCY

33, OLD BOND STREET, LONDON, W.

Who will be pleased to play over records at any time without obligation to purchase.

McCormack recorded about eighty sides for Odeon. Marketing however, was not the company's forte and his celebrity as a recording artist would not have reached the heights it did had he remained with them.

switched from companies that made cylinders to disc manufacturers and vice versa. More likely, his decision was based on the terms he was offered.

Had the Gramophone & Typewriter Co. taken the trouble to hear McCormack, they might have been agreeably surprised at the progress he had made since going to Italy. Arthur Brooks of the Odeon Company auditioned the young tenor and showed better judgement, promptly signing him to an exclusive recording contract for six years at £150 per year. Between 1906 and 1909 (when his contract was bought out), McCormack recorded about eighty sides for the Odeon Company. These are fascinating vocal documents, demonstrating the rapid development of both vocal technique and personality that McCormack made in these formative years. In the

53

It was a common practice for Odeon artists to inscribe the original wax recording or 'positive' with their signature. On the disk 'The Bay of Biscay', McCormack went further. Beneath his signature, he appears to have written 'badly arranged'. The word 'badly' was then scratched out.

first of the records, the voice is predictably stronger and the range more extensive than in 1904, but there is a self-consciousness in the care he takes in moulding and 'knitting' the legato line, with the words remaining correspondingly unimportant. His vowel sounds are sometimes capricious. By 1908, he comes across as more confident and there is a greater spontaneity in his approach. The following year, his last with the Odeon Company, the increased range can nearly be taken for granted, there is more to the vocal personality, words are savoured.

Recording contracts were one thing, getting concert engagements another. Almost as soon as McCormack had arrived in London, he got an introduction to the Bernhardt Brothers who ran a West End concert agency – the Philharmonic Concert Direction – at 82 Regent Street. He appears to have accepted an exclusive contract with alacrity, even though the brothers were not in the kind of business that McCormack most wanted. But work was work and he was provided with immediate employment in Brighton, Portsmouth and other provincial English towns. Henry Bernhardt promoted concerts of his own, most notably Sunday concerts on the Palace Pier, Brighton, with performances twice daily, once in the afternoon and once in the evening, with the same artists appearing twice. McCormack was taken on as an assisting artist.

The stars of light musicals and musical comedy topped the bill, Lily Langtry and Gertie Millar among them. And, on one occasion, McCormack appeared on the same bill as the sensational Camille Clifford renowned for her hourglass figure and romance in high places. Other artists that appeared in Brighton, with perhaps less notable figures but with higher musical standing, included the violinist Joseph Szigeti (1892–1973) starting out on his career; the Irish bass-baritone Harry Plunket-

Greene (1865–1936) and the popular Australian baritone Peter Dawson (1882–1961). Greene never had much of a voice but was a sensitive artist who was the first singer to give Schumann's *Dicterliebe* complete and unabridged in London and who, over a ten-year period of giving concerts in the capital, is said to have never repeated a single item. He was noted for his fine diction, a feature of his work, and of Dawson's, that would surely have made an impression on McCormack.

Using his Italian name of Giovanni Foli, McCormack sang his first concert for Bernhardt on Brighton Pier on 9th September 1906, thereafter he reverted to J F McCormack. He returned to Dublin to sing with the Dublin Oratorio and Choral Society at the Rotunda Round Room on 7th November. Vincent O'Brien was the conductor and McCormack sang in the 'Misere' from *Il Trovatore* and the 'Brindisi' from *La Traviata*. *Il Trovatore* was hardly an opera that suited McCormack, but it was all grist to the mill. He was back singing in Brighton just a few days later, on 11th November, and crossed again to Dublin to appear at a 'Grand Charity Concert' at the Theatre Royal on 28th November, when he sang 'O Amore' from Mascagni's opera *L'Amico Fritz*, Leoni's 'In Sympathy' and, in the third act, the duet 'Parigi, O Cara' from *La Traviata* in which he was partnered by soprano Fanny Bauer. Joseph O'Mara was the leading figure in this concert and the accompanists were Vincent O'Brien and J F Larchet. Before the month was out, McCormack was back in Brighton and, over the ensuing months, sang in some of the larger provincial towns. Bernhardt, not one to undersell his artists, spoke in advance publicity of 'the wonderful young Irish tenor, about whom everyone is talking in London, and who is to appear at the Royal Opera next month'. McCormack had no such engagement and his approaches to Covent Garden had been turned down.

An offer came his way from the Moody-Manners Opera Company but, for one reason or another, nothing came of it. Lily says John was offered £8 and wanted to hold out for £10. Charles Manners pointed out that the tenor had little experience, and his acting was not on the same level as his singing. McCormack is said to have replied that, if this had been so, he would be singing at Covent Garden. In his 1992 article in *The Record Collector*, 'McCormack on Brighton Pier', John Ward writes: 'This reply suggests that money was not the real issue for him. His ambitions were firmly focused upon the Royal Opera House and an engagement with a provincial touring company would have been in his own eyes a failure.' However, he had already auditioned for the musical *Waltz Dream*, for which he had been rejected. This was a work under the management of George Edwardes, regarded as being responsible for 'the invention or discovery of Musical Comedy', and famed for the statuesque Edwardian beauties he employed, the so-called Gaiety Girls. To audition for work in this milieu does not suggest a singer too pernickety about where his next meal might come from. But this would have enabled McCormack to stay in London where his ambitions lay, whereas touring with Charles Manners would not.

If a letter he wrote from Torrington Square on 26th September 1906 is anything to go by, in the midst of rebuffs, McCormack continued to seek out work on his own, not relying on the Bernhardt Brothers.

> Dear Mrs Beddington,
>
> I thank you so much for your kind letters and for being so good as to write to Tosti again on my behalf.
> I have just written to him asking him to make an appointment to hear me.
> You will be glad to hear that I am getting on very well here in London. Madame Liza Lehmann heard me and immediately engaged me for her opera, *The Vicar of Wakefield*, with David Bispham as baritone, and this week I am to be heard by Mr Harry Higgins of Covent Garden, in view of a prospective engagement.
> Thanking you for all your kindly interest and that you will 'put in a kind word for me when you can',
>
> I remain
> Yours truly
> J F McCormack

The upbeat style of the letter was not, however, matched by what was going on in his career. According to John Ward, there is no evidence that Paolo Tosti did anything for McCormack or if he even interviewed him. *The Vicar of Wakefield* was a world premiere and, as such, would have been an important engagement. Raymond Foxall in *John McCormack* claimed that:

> A *Sunday Express* writer said in later years that he had once been shown a letter sacking McCormack in 1906 from the cast of *The Vicar of Wakefield*. With the letter had been a cheque for £20 to pay him off. 'He had not turned up for rehearsals,' said the writer, 'and in any case no one seemed then to think much of him.'

It seems highly unlikely that McCormack missed rehearsals. He was known for reliability throughout his career. David Bispham, who as well as taking the title role in the opera was also the producer, recalled in *A Quaker Singer's Recollections*:

I had trouble in finding a tenor for the part... and was about to engage Walter Hyde when Madame Lehmann begged me first to hear a young man whose voice had been brought to her attention. Accordingly, one Sunday afternoon in September 1906, I went with my conductor, the late Hamish MacCunn, and my manager, Bram Stoker, so long Sir Henry Irving's right-hand man, to Madame Lehmann's house at Wimbledon, where we heard several selections beautifully rendered by a young Irishman named John McCormack. After he had sung, my dear Liza took me into the next room and enthusiastically said, 'David, if you don't engage him you're a fool. He has an angel's voice.' 'True,' said I, 'but he has an Irishman's brogue.' 'He can get over that,' said she fervently. 'Send him to Richard Temple for lessons.' This famous artist, after years at the Savoy Theatre, upon Sir Arthur Sullivan's death became a professor of spoken English in the Royal College of Music.

I presently took McCormack aside and said, 'If I engage you for this part, you must try to get over your brogue.' 'Sure,' he said, in his delightful way, 'it's no matter at all – at all! Oliver Goldsmith was born just two mile over the hill from where I came from.' 'True,' I replied, 'I know Oliver Goldsmith was an Irishman; but he wrote an English story, and it will never do for you to play the part of Squire Thornhill with a brogue.'

Though Mr McCormack accepted the part, he found it unsuitable and soon returned it.

In the event, the role was taken by the English tenor Walter Hyde (1875–1951) who had already made a success in the musical *My Lady Molly*. Ironically, Hyde was not to make it to Covent Garden until a year after McCormack had made his debut there.

The tenor *did* miss an engagement, another Palace Pier concert scheduled for 31st March 1907, but this time there was no talk of being absent without leave. He had crossed to Dublin to see his first-born child, Cyril Patrick, who had arrived on 27th March. 'I shall never forget his face when the nurse asked him if he would like to hold his son in his arms,' Lily remembered. 'He said, "I was scared stiff to touch the baby, but sure I had had no experience of fatherhood." He put his hands together gently like a cup and held them out. I wish I had a picture of the two of them then.' Cyril's sister Gwen arrived a year later to complete the McCormack household.

McCormack moved between London and Dublin quite frequently during the first year or so of settling in London. His main objective was to sing at Covent

McCormack in Gounod's Faust which he sang in Dublin with the Dublin Amateur Operatic Society under the direction of another Irish tenor, Barton McGuckin. 'I thought no tenor could ever look so stunning as mine did in his costume of deep purple velvet and mauve satin trimmed with silver lace,' Lily recalled.

Garden but, while that remained beyond his reach, he took engagements where and when he could. He was back in Dublin again in May 1907 to sing in *Cavalleria Rusticana* and *Faust* with the Dublin Amateur Operatic Society under the direction of Barton McGuckin. Whatever he may have been paid – no doubt it was small – it was important for him to get stage experience. And to get to sing the role of Turiddu in *Cavalleria Rusticana* was to prove fortuitous.

The reference in the letter to Mrs Beddington to the upcoming audition at the Royal Opera, Covent Garden, came to nothing. And McCormack must have realised early on that the Bernhardt agency was not suitable for the kind of singer he wanted to become or the work he wanted to do. The exclusive contract might well be found invalid today. Getting out of it then was a costly exercise. Pierre Key in *John McCormack: His Own Life Story* records a conversation he had with Michael Keane, the American representative for Boosey & Company:

> Shortly after McCormack came to London upon finishing his studies in Italy, he made a contract with a London agent. The boy was inexperienced in the ways of business, and being generous himself he did not question the equity of the contract which might be drawn for him to sign…
>
> Some idea of the character of this contract may be gathered from the fact that it was for the duration of McCormack's life. Fancy such an arrangement. Of course it couldn't last. Yet the cancellation of that document cost the tenor, years afterwards, ten thousand dollars.

It is certainly true that Bernhardt had put work in McCormack's way when he was most in need of it, but the most important contacts appear to have been of his own making. He needed money but, at the beginning of 1907, engagements were not plentiful. In February, he got an appearance at the Choughs Musical Society at the Cannon Street Hotel. A week later he sang at the Rotunda in Dublin and returned to London for a Thomas Moore Memorial Concert held by the Irish Club in Charing Cross Road on 15th February. Dennis O'Sullivan, he of the leonine voice, also sang but, 'No individual vocalist,' declared *The Weekly Freeman*, '…scored a greater success than Mr J F McCormack.' This concert proved to be an important one for, on the strength of it, he was engaged by Henry Mills, secretary of the Sunday National League, to sing on 17th February at a National League concert at Queen's Hall, supporting the violinist Marie Hall. The following day, again through Mills, McCormack sang at the Alexander Palace with the band of the Scots Guards. If he, with his republican sympathies, saw any irony in being accompanied by a British military band, it is not recorded.

Silk programme for a performance of Carmen *and* Cavalleria Rusticana *given by the Dublin Amateur Operatic Society on 13th May 1907, with McCormack in the role of Turiddu. Although the company was an amateur one, the luxury of a silk programme can be explained by the fact that the event was 'under the Patronage and Presence of His Excellency the Lord Lieutenant' as noted at the top of the programme.*

Theatre Royal,
DUBLIN.

MR. FREDK. MOUILLOT ... ... Managing Director.
MR. GEORGE PARRINGTON ... ... Resident Manager.
THE DUBLIN THEATRE CO., LTD. ... ... Proprietors.

MONDAY, MAY 13th, 1907.
Under the Patronage and Presence of
HIS EXCELLENCY
THE LORD LIEUTENANT.

DUBLIN AMATEUR OPERATIC SOCIETY.
SECOND SEASON.

— SECOND ACT OF —
CARMEN.

CARMEN	-	-	-	MISS TESSA BYRNE
FRASQUITA				MRS. J. J. FAGAN
MERCEDES				MISS LILIAN FLOOD
DON JOZE				MR. W. H. JONES
ESCAMILO				MR. SIDNEY HARALD
ZUNIGA				MR. WILLIAM CLARK
MORALES				MR. G. R. SMITH
IL DANCAIRO				MR. EUGENE LEAHY
IL REMENDADO				MR. CHARLES MEYERS
LILIAS PASTIA				MR. L. R. CAREY

ACT 2 ... ... THE PASARDA OF LILIAS PASTIA

FOLLOWED BY MASCAGNI'S
"CAVALLERIA RUSTICANA."

SAUTUZZA	-	-	-	MRS. STELLA BOWMAN
LOLA				MISS TESSA BYRNE
LUCIA				MISS MAY DURKIN
ALFIO				MR. ERNEST CAMERON
TURRIDU				MR. J. F. McCORMACK

SCENE - - - - A SQUARE IN A VILLAGE IN SICILY.

Mesdames:—Armstrong, Alexander, Beardwood, Browne, Cooney, Doyle, Dillon, Elson, Fagan, Galway, Hammond, Jones, Leech, McCullagh, Nolan, O'Connor, O'Connell, Ryan, Stanley.
Mesdemoiselles:—Allan, Ahearne, Brady, Bradley, R. Barry, T. Byrne, O. Barry, Bagg, A. Byrne, E. Byrne, M. Clarke, T. Carter, C. Cullen, Canty, Donnelly, Durkin, Dowling, Daly, Edwardes, A. Fitzpatrick, L. Fitzpatrick, A. Fagan, L. Flood, Geoghegan, Griffth, Galvin, Hackett, Harte, Hannan, Hartigan, Hogan, Kenny, N. Kerrin, M. Kerrin, Kearney, Kitson, Lee, Latimer, Leeson, Lennon, Lalor, G. Murray, L. Murray, O. Murray, Moran, McLean, McMullen, McDowell, F. McDonald, E. McDonald, McCabe, Nugent, Norton, Neale, Naughton, O'Connor, O'Sullivan, A. M. Pelissier, M. A. Pelissier, Quirke, D. Reddy, E. Reddy, Ryan, M. Smyth, Toner, K. Walsh, K. Weinstock, A. Whelan, etc., etc.
Messieurs:—Braniboll, Browner, G. Byrne, P. Brady, G. Brady, N. Byrne, Baker, Coldwell, Carey, W. Clarke, Cameron, Crawley, F. Clarke, Crowley, Dowling, Elson, Eustace, Ellard, Fitzpatrick, Godkin, Gorman, Harold, Harding, Harrisson, Hughes, Ireland, Jones, Kenny, Lurring, Layng, Lockett, Leahy, Meredith, Mulcahy, Montgomery, Murray, Munro, Meyer, Meyer, Bolson, McNevin, McCormack, McCarthy, O'Mahony, O'Reilly, Odbert, Pollaaier, Pierce, Ryan, Richardson, Ryder, Stewart, Somers, Swan, Stanley, C. R. Smith, G. W. Smith, Tyner, A. T. Walsh, Walker, J. Walsh, Whelan, etc., etc.
Costumes and Wigs by Clarkson, London, Costumier and Perruquier to His Majesty the King. Dances arranged by Miss Eithne Magee.

CHORUS OF 200. LARGELY AUGMENTED ORCHESTRA.

MUSICAL DIRECTOR ... ... MR. BARTON McGUCKIN
Stage Manager ... ... MR. H. BROOKLYN
Honorary Secretary ... Mr. C. R. SMITH, 14 D'OLIER ST., DUBLIN

His concert engagements were picking up pace. Through Alberto Visetti, a singing teacher and one time accompanist of Adelina Patti, McCormack got letters of introduction to William Boosey of Chappells and Arthur Boosey of Boosey & Company, cousins and rivals in the music publishing business. Boosey had originally dealt in continental opera scores; but, in a costly lawsuit, it was ruled that Boosey had no copyright over such material. As a result, the company went into the publishing of new ballads and songs. The move proved lucrative. In support of this new line of business, Boosey took to promoting ballad concerts, first at St James's Hall and, when it was demolished for development, at the Queen's Hall, which had been built in 1893. (It was destroyed by Luftwaffe bombing in 1941.) This was still the heyday of the music hall and of the drawing-room ballad when, it was said, everyone had a piano and no one a gramophone. People would come along to hear new songs and then go off and buy the sheet music so that they could play and sing the pieces at home. It should not be thought that because these were ballad concerts they were somehow second rate. On one occasion William Boosey recalled:

> ...a noted prima donna wrote me a most indignant letter, because a brilliant light-opera artiste appeared in the same pro-gramme as herself! I wrote and said I regretted her distress, but that at all events the light-opera artiste sang absolutely in tune. I heard no more.

McCormack first went to Chappells and, on presenting himself, was told William Boosey was out. He then went to Boosey and seemingly had a loss of nerve. Expecting another rebuff, he walked off. When Arthur Boosey sent for him, he was nowhere to be found. However, a meeting was arranged later and the publisher took an instant liking to McCormack. It was Arthur Boosey, Lily reckoned, who started off John's delight in collecting old scores:

> Arthur Boosey was always kind and considerate to John. Among other favours, he allowed him to have bundles of music taken down from dusty shelves which had been undisturbed for years. That started John's craze for 'digging' as he called it. In every town he and Teddy Schneider [his accompanist] would spend hours on end going over old, faded manuscripts in the music shops. In this way he discovered some lovely Handel and Mozart arias and also violin and piano pieces, which he would present to his musician friends – gems which they didn't even know

existed. When he set his mind to find a particular piece of music he wouldn't give in until he got it.

His breadth of repertoire, what he sang in public concerts and privately at home far exceeded what we can ever know. He constantly expanded his concert repertoire but little enough of it was committed to disc.

It was also Arthur Boosey who suggested that the tenor drop the 'J F' and present himself simply as John McCormack; and Boosey offered him an appearance at the very next Boosey ballad concert for 1st March 1907. Apart from featuring some of the finest oratorio and opera singers and recitalists of the day, these concerts were also a platform for newcomers. 'It is important to find the right new song for the right new singer,' commented William Boosey in *Fifty Years of Music*. 'It is not so easy to make a success as a newcomer at a ballad concert and principally for the reason that you have only three or four minutes on the platform, during which time you have got to get hold of your audience. Of course some newcomers are lucky enough to have a new song in readiness for their first appearance which is absolutely adapted to their style.'

McCormack had exactly that. His accompanist for the concert was the composer Samuel Liddle who offered him his new song 'A Farewell', a setting of a poem by Charles Kingsley. The sentiments, a father's farewell message to his child, are exactly the kind of thing that had appeal in Victorian and Edwardian days. McCormack made an immediate impression with the ballad, which went on to become a popular drawing-room ballad of the day. He recorded it twice, in 1908 and 1912, its gentle, limpid phrases and plaintive lyrics suiting McCormack's voice and temperament well. His singing is typically direct and heartfelt and, like so many songs, he draws us into 'A Farewell' as if into a confidence.

Not every critic was won over, however. Francis Toye recalled in his autobiography, *For What We Have Received*, what he had written at the time of that concert – ruefully as it was a judgement so wide of the mark: 'There was a new tenor called McCormack with lots of voice but no brains.' Lacking brains was not an issue raised again. The directness of his style and his youthful verve may have seemed naïve to Toye as the finely judged performances of the mature artist were yet to come. Nevertheless, naïve or not, after this debut McCormack became a regular performer at the Boosey ballad concerts. At the same time, the drawing rooms of fashionable Edwardian England were opening up to him. Perceval Graves retained a vivid memory of the ageing Duchess of Devonshire, something of a judge of voices (albeit with the aid of a hearing trumpet) delighting in McCormack's ringing rendition of Stephen Adams' impassioned ballad 'Roses'. The duchess judged him to be 'a natural with tremendous conviction'. Graves adds:

The old lady was so delighted that she told all her friends and influential acquaintances all about the young minstrel, who soon became swamped with lucrative engagements.

And even before he had left his meagre lodgings in Torrington Square, McCormack was to be offered the song with which he is inseparably associated even to this day, and whose title Lily used for her biography of her husband. Composers were always looking for singers who might promote their work. Perceval Graves remembered opening the door to Charles Marshall:

> ...who gave his name rather diffidently, with a request to meet McCormack who, luckily, happened to be at home, as he said: 'I have a song here which I think will suit him.' At that time Marshall was a struggling song-writer, a shade over fifty. Much encouraged by John's cordial reception, he sat down and played it over once and then McCormack sang it. After the first line, he became enthusiastic. 'It's great. You must come with me at once to meet Mr Arthur Boosey. He is sure to take it.' And he did.

But not without some persuasion. McCormack, however, had no doubts and his instincts were proved right. He introduced the song – 'I Hear You Calling Me' – at a Boosey ballad concert, and thereafter sang it wherever he went. To all intents and purposes, it was *his* song and its popularity was reflected in the enormous record royalties it brought him. Sad to say, Marshall made little out of his famous song.

McCormack lost no time in recording 'I Hear You Calling Me' for the Odeon Company twice in 1908, first with piano accompaniment by the composer and then with orchestral backing. There were no less than six versions of the song published. In all, McCormack repeated it for the Victor Company in America in 1910, again in 1911, then in 1921 and, finally, he made an electric version in 1927. In addition, in 1929, it was one of the songs he recorded for the film *Song O' My Heart*. The two Odeon recordings are attractive for their youthfulness and are self-conscious to a point, the text relatively unnoticed in relation to the melodic line. By 1911, McCormack can take his vocal technique for granted, the voice is perfectly equalised and the legato beautifully controlled. But he makes much more of the song in the 1927 version, where he paces the song to draw out its meaning to the full, savouring the words, reaching out to his unseen audience. Not only does the vocal line enchant, it is impossible to think of the song without hearing his hauntingly beautiful rendering of the lines:

'Though years have stretched their weary lengths between/ And on your grave the mossy grass is green/ … I hear you calling me.'

It was quite possible in Edwardian London to make a living from concerts and, by 1907, McCormack was making his way financially. It was time to get Lily and baby Cyril over from Dublin to join him. The lodgings in Torrington Square were not suitable for a family of three and he lost no time in finding something better. He wrote to Lily saying that he had found just the thing in 16 Cricklade Avenue, on Streatham Hill, conveniently near the railway station, a small house in a modest terrace. 'This was the one short period in his life when he was *not* extravagant,' Lily recalled. He set about furnishing it himself. He wanted to have a nest all set up for his wife and child by the time they joined him. 'I suggested,' wrote Lily, 'that he might like me over for a few days to help him, but he would have none of that. I could see that he was determined to do it alone and all that was required of me was to be pleased and surprised!' She was. Having been met by John at Charing Cross Station, they made straight for their new home. 'The excitement was so intense I don't remember how we got to Streatham Hill – by taxi or train… Outside it was just another little house in an avenue of houses, but inside – ah, that was another story.' It is not difficult to imagine Lily's surprise when:

> A young maid in cap and apron opened the door. John had arranged every detail with such care that I was almost speechless. I recall that I particularly had to admire a large Japanese cabinet in the drawing room, which he proudly explained had been a real bargain at a sale… it was all perfection to us. It seemed particularly marvellous to me not having to find a place to live, and then struggle to furnish it, although I found out in due course that John had to struggle terrifically to pay for it all, especially the baby grand piano, which took up most of the drawing room!

After Cyril had been put down in his cot, and John and Lily sat down for dinner, he turned to her and said proudly: 'You see, I haven't forgotten a thing, even to the salt!'

The engagement McCormack most desired was now about to come his way. He had been heard at one of the Sunday League Concerts by Sir John Murray Scott, an establishment figure who had considerable wealth and influence and who lived with his two sisters, the Misses Mary and Alicia Scott, in considerable luxury and in the midst of a fine art and furniture collection at 5 Connaught Place. Into this household, John and later Lily (who was still in Dublin with her baby when the connection was first made) were welcomed; and it was through Sir John Murray Scott, more than anyone else, that McCormack became familiar with the ways of Edwardian

John and Lily
on the steps of
5 Auburn Terrace,
Athone, with Cyril,
and Andrew and
Hannah McCormack.

McCormack
looking rather
meek in the
presence of his
benefactor Sir
John Murray Scott.
Scott, a man of
immense wealth,
was John and
Lily's entrée into
Edwardian high
society.

society, and developed a taste for the life of the English aristocracy that he was later to emulate. Lily recalled her first afternoon tea at Connaught Place:

> I was happy to be asked but I realised that I was going to be 'vetted'. They were already so interested in John that I knew they would naturally be curious to see for themselves what kind of a girl he had married — when he seemed far too young to be married at all. John had no suspicion how nervous I was, but in a short while I felt I had cleared the first fence at least, Miss Alicia and Miss Mary were cordial and charming, and before we left asked if they might call on us the following week and see the baby. Both sisters were sweet and motherly, and Miss Mary became a kind of guardian angel to us both. From the start I felt that I had real friends behind me and had only to ask them if I had the slightest doubt about anything. London society in those days made many demands and to be plunged into it young and inexperienced as we were was a serious matter for us.

Knowing how much the young tenor had set his heart on singing at Covent Garden, Sir John Murray Scott arranged an audition with Harry Higgins, then general manager of the opera house. According to Lily's account, after John had sung, Higgins gave his opinion that his voice was too small for so large an auditorium. Murray Scott, who had sat in on the audition, is then said to have retorted that if the orchestra played more softly then all the singers could be heard!

That seemed to be the end of the matter but, a short time later, McCormack was asked if he could deputise for an indisposed tenor in *Rigoletto*. Unfortunately, he had not studied the role of the Duke of Mantua and there was no time available for him to learn it. So the opportunity to sing in the Grand Summer Season of 1907 passed him by.

However, this disappointment was followed by an offer to sing the role of Turiddu in Mascagni's *Cavalleria Rusticana* in the Autumn Season. And so, at twenty-three, McCormack became the youngest tenor ever to sing a major role at the Royal Opera. On the day of the performance, 15th October 1907, McCormack ran through his role with the opera house's *répétiteur*, while Sir John Murray Scott, 'looking after him like a father', insisted that he had lunch at his house, to be followed by a rest in the afternoon. A carriage was then ready to take him the short distance to the opera house. Before leaving Connaught Place, McCormack put through a call to Lily for luck. It would be difficult to know which of them was the more nervous:

The façade of the Royal Opera House, Covent Garden, around the turn of the twentieth century.

Aunty [Lily's sister Peggy Foley who became a much-loved part of the McCormack household] and I, with the rest of the family [who had come over from Ireland] had seats in the fifth row stalls, centre. John had seen to that. I wore my new gown of pale pink pleated chiffon with a band of silver brocade in my hair. I can't describe my jewels – I hadn't any. How well I remember wishing that I could get under the seat and listen from there, instead of having to sit in full view of the audience, wondering if I would faint when the curtain went up. I don't believe I have ever prayed harder that I did that night and I must say my prayers were answered.

A sizeable contingent of Irishmen living in London were assembled in advance of the opera, ready to cheer their man to the rafters. Perceval Graves was among them:

It was for me a wildly exciting night. Two hundred and fifty of us marched from the old Irish Club in Charing Cross Road to

Covent Garden, marshalled by old Sam Goddes, the proprietor, to form a powerful Hibernian claque. The Italian claques were powerful enough up there during the Italian season, so why not an

Royal Opera Covent Garden
Lessee and Manager ... Mr. FRANK RENDLE
Autumn Opera Season, 1907
Mr. FRANK RENDLE
in conjunction with
{ THE GRAND OPERA SYNDICATE, LTD.
General Manager, Mr. NEIL FORSYTH
Musical Director, Mr. PERCY PITT }

THIS EVENING'S PERFORMANCE

Saturday, October 26th, at 8
MASCAGNI'S Opera
CAVALLERIA RUSTICANA
(IN ITALIAN)

Turiddu	... ...	Mr. JOHN McCORMACK
Alfio ...	... ...	Signor SCANDIANI
Lola ...	... ...	Signora ZOFFOLI
Lucia ...	... ...	Signora BORGHI
Santuzza	...	Mlle. PRYHN
Conductor	...	Signor PANIZZA

Followed by LEONCAVALLO'S Opera
PAGLIACCI
(IN ITALIAN)

Nedda	... ...	Mlle. DE LIS
Canio	... ..	Signor BASSI
Tonio	... ...	Signor SAMMARCO
Beppe	... ...	Signor BADA
Silvio ...	... ..	Mr. ALBERT GARCIA
Conductor	...	Signor PANIZZA

Programme for Cavalleria Rusticana *in which McCormack made his Covent Garden debut on 26th October 1907, at twenty-three the youngest tenor ever to sing a major role there.*

Irish contingent? I can't remember where we all sat but I distinctly recollect the hush that fell over the audience when, with the curtain down and the house dark, we listened intently for the first notes of the deathless Siciliana, from the moment the strains began to filter through the curtain to the expectant audience to the end of the aria. And we realized that another star had arrived, no meteor either, but a planet that would beam brightly and steadfastly in the musical firmament. That top C of his, whether ringing out with a silver resonance or subdued to a delicate *mezza voce*, was unsurpassable. Of his acting, it is kinder to say nothing except that he was just himself, a simple and sincere Irish singer, incapable of interpreting the Sicilian way of life.

The support of the Irish brigade did not go unnoticed in the press. The *Daily Telegraph* noted that, although the opera had already been presented in this season:

> …there was a house of far larger dimensions than before. And not only was the assembled multitude greater, their enthusiasm was on a par, and the scene at the close of the first-named [i.e. *Cavalleria Rusticana* which was paired, as is traditional, with Leoncavallo's *Pagliacci*] was one not often witnessed in our chief opera house. We need not stop to argue as to how much or how little of this was due to love of the operas themselves. If it was in support of Mr John McCormack, a young Irish singer of great promise, who as Turiddu took his first operatic plunge, who shall hold up his hand against it?

A highly strung performer at the best of times, one can only imagine the torture of nerves that McCormack must have endured at this debut. It did not go unnoticed. *The Times* spoke of 'the weakness of his first entrance' and that he showed his inexperience: '…by strolling about the stage and allowing himself ineffective actions. Moreover, in the first act the quality of his voice did not compare well with that of Mlle Bryhn [who played Santuzza].' However by the time the second act arrived, McCormack had settled his nerves somewhat so that he appeared 'more at ease and he used his voice with admirable effect'.

A mere three weeks later, on 6th November 1907, McCormack sang the role of Don Ottavio in Mozart's *Don Giovanni*. This is not a role that makes the same kind of dramatic demands on a singer as Turiddu, but it does require singing of high technical finish. It was exactly what McCormack was able to deliver, so much so that

The Times described his performance as: 'A great success; the songs – both of them were given – were sung with fine taste and vocal finish, while the timbre of the voice is exactly what is wanted in the part.' The *Daily Telegraph* noted that 'it is easy to say [he] has much to learn', presumably in reference to his stagecraft, but singled out his rendering of 'Dalla sua pace' as having been given 'with a sense of phrasing that was exquisite'.

The Don Giovanni on this occasion was the Sicilian baritone Mario Sammarco (1873–1930). He made a tremendous impression in the role and was a firm favourite in London. He and McCormack were to be associated in many other performances at Covent Garden and elsewhere and made a number of records together, including 'O Mimi, tu più non torni' from Puccini's *La Bohème* and 'Del tempio al limitar' from Bizet's *I Pescatori di Perle*. These two discs made a special impression on the American critic, Henry Pleasants, who wrote of them:

> On none of these early recordings is the voice of the young
> McCormack heard more ideally than in the two duets with
> Mario Sammarco. His upper voice then [1910–11] was freer than
> it would be later on, and he attacks the A-flats and B-flats with an
> exultant ease. The two B-flats in the duet from *The Pearl Fishers*
> – especially the coldly attacked first of them – eight measures
> before the end – are as thrillingly and lyrically perfect as any in
> the entire catalog of tenor recording.

Inside two appearances at Covent Garden, McCormack had made his mark – an extraordinary achievement given his age and inexperience. And he was about to part- ner one of the greatest sopranos of the time, Luisa Tetrazzini (1871–1940). She was a seasoned campaigner with an immense reputation in South America and in Italy, but was unknown in London. Her unheralded appearance at Covent Garden, a month after McCormack's own debut, was to a half-empty house on a dismal wet evening, yet her coloratura singing created a furore. If Nellie Melba, the reigning *prima donna assoluta* at Covent Garden, saw the heading in *The Spectator*, she could not have been pleased – it announced: 'The re-emergence of the prima donna', and the article went on to bemoan the fact that it mattered not at all what opera was put on, only so long as Luisa Tetrazzini was in it. Everyone now wanted to hear her, to the point that, as *The Graphic* noted on 23rd November, the same month as she had arrived:

> So astounding has been the success of Mme Tetrazzini that I
> understand that the Covent Garden authorities have been com-
> pelled to pass a new rule to the effect that early galleryites, district

Signed photograph
of the great
coloratura soprano
Luisa Tetrazzini
(1871–1940),
taken in London
in 1908. She took
a great liking to
McCormack and
he called her his
'fairy godmother'.
She drove audi-
ences to a frenzy
of excitement with
her pyrotechnics
and scintillating
top notes.

messenger boys, and all others whom it may concern, may not on any consideration take up their places outside the doors before midday. The congestion in Floral Street was... becoming a positive nuisance, and such was the competition among Tetrazzini-ites for the honour of being first in the field, that there seemed to be every possibility that, before long, they would be taking their breakfast there, as well as their lunch, tea and dinner.

No voice and no kind of singing provokes hysteria among an audience so much as a coloratura, and Tetrazzini could throw off high Cs and higher with an insouciance that was sensational. That McCormack should be invited to partner Tetrazzini was a boon to his own career. If he had not known the role of the Duke of Mantua during summer, he certainly knew it by the autumn. Tetrazzini and McCormack sang together for the first time in *Rigoletto* on 23rd November 1907. The tearaway duke was not a role that McCormack had the temperament to portray on stage, and *The Graphic*, when he repeated the role the following year, noted that he made 'a somewhat respectable roué'. Too respectable perhaps for Tetrazzini. Always susceptible to a good-looking male, she took a special interest in her new tenor. Maybe she was making a quip but, on one occasion, she suggested that the pair of them run away together. 'But I have a wife and two children,' McCormack protested. 'Well, you can bring the children,' Tet replied.

Nellie Melba, the Australian prima donna, would never have made such a remark to McCormack. Quite apart from the fact that Melba was more interested in titled lovers, there was no love lost between her and McCormack although their professional relationship was to extend over three continents. They got off to a bad start. When McCormack followed Melba out on stage for their curtain calls, she waved him back with the comment, 'No one takes a bow with Melba.' No name is mentioned in Mrs Claude Beddington's autobiography, *All That I Have Met*, but there can be little doubt that Melba is the singer in question in the following:

> McCormack – in common with almost every other singer of the day – disliked intensely a certain elderly *diva*. One night his wife and I went on to the stage at Covent Garden at the end of an opera in which John and this lady had been singing impassioned love-songs, both singly and together. Said John to me: 'D'ye know that I was in me perambulator when that woman made her debut?... an' while we have our arms round one another an' singin' love-duets, says she to me: 'John, I wish ye was in hell!'... Says I: 'I wouldn't mind the way *you* weren't there!'

73

The Australian soprano Nellie Melba (1861–1931) as Violetta in La Traviata. *She had a remarkably long career, making her debut at Covent Garden in 1888, when McCormack was only four years old, and continued to sing there until 1926, a span of thirty-eight years.*

For all that, there were few sopranos McCormack admired as much as Melba. Her voice was sometimes likened to that of a choirboy for its purity, a quality it retained almost to the end of a remarkably long career. She was McCormack's senior by twenty-three years. He was her tenor in Puccini's *La Bohème* on 22nd May 1913 when she celebrated her twenty-fifth season at Covent Garden. He wrote: 'It must always be reckoned amongst the great events of my life. I had the honour of being Rudolfo. I

never witnessed such a demonstration. It was a splendid tribute to a marvellous woman and incomparable artist. I believe – in fact, I know – that I sing better with Melba than with any other soprano… It is an inspiration.'

Nor, of course, was there any love lost between Melba and Tetrazzini. Melba rather looked upon Covent Garden as her own preserve and did not take kindly to rivals coming upon her pitch. Melba was much more than merely a singer or even a prima donna. She was part of the establishment, boasted of having been kissed on both cheeks by any number of royalty, and had a close relationship with those that mattered at Covent Garden including Lady de Grey and Neil Forsythe, the general manager – not to mention Harry Higgins, chairman of the Grand Opera Syndicate. Higgins was Lady de Grey's brother-in-law and Forsythe was related to Higgins. Little wonder then if this cosy relationship was much to Melba's advantage. Her influence held sway. When she chose McCormack to be her tenor at Covent Garden for the first time, he was summoned to Forsythe's office and solemnly informed of the honour. When McCormack enquired as to whether this meant a raise for him, he was informed, no doubt with equal solemnity, that it did not. To be asked to attend one of Nellie Melba's parties was regarded as something of an honour. Lily recalled:

> Mme Melba's party, given on the night of one of the court balls
> during the opera season, was a revelation to me – the ladies in
> their presentation gowns of wonderful brocades and rare laces
> and jewels beyond all description, and the men in court dress

75

with decorations or vivid uniforms. Melba herself looked as if she had stepped out of the ballroom scene in *Traviata* in a robe of flesh-pink satin with flounces of priceless lace, a wonderful tiara, and all her famous jewels.

My gown, which had been made by the Misses Scotts' court dressmaker specially for the great occasion, was emerald green satin (so tight waisted that I could scarcely breath), trimmed lavishly with Limerick lace. I realise now that it was more for a woman of fifty than one in her early twenties, but John said he was proud of me that night. It was considered a great honour to John and me to be invited to that party, as 'Nellie' was known to be very sparing with her invitations to fellow artists, especially such young ones.

It is said that it was through Melba's influence that the Viennese soprano Selma Kurz was kept away from the Royal Opera, along with others, including the delightful Geraldine Farrar with whom McCormack would sing in America. Tetrazzini had got in through the back door, so to speak, during the Autumn Season, when Melba was on tour in Australia. Melba was back the following year, however, and the ensuing rivalry was much to the delight of *The Spectator:*

Some say, compared with Tetrazzini
That Melba's voice is shrill and tinny,
While those who Madame Melba laud,
Think Tetrazzini quite a fraud.
Strange that such difference there should be
'Twixt Tweedledum and Tweedledee.

What goes round comes round. This little jingle would appear to be a take on a much earlier one by John Byrum in 1724 comparing George Friderick Handel with his great rival Giovanni Bononcini:

Some say, compared to Bononcini,
That Myn Heer Handel's but a ninny;
Others aver that he to Handel
Is scarcely fit to hold a Candle.
Strange all this difference should be
'Twixt Tweedle-dum and Tweedle-dee.

The Graphic, equally tongue in cheek, suggested in 1908 that: 'There is no reason to suppose… that the rivalry between Mme Tetrazzini and Mme Melba will be anything but friendly, and certainly an opportunity of contrasting their methods should prove exceedingly interesting.'

STARS IN OPPOSITION; OR, THE "RECORD" OPERATIC DUEL.

Cartoon from The Illustrated London News *depicting an 'operatic duel' between Tetrazzini and Melba. Ironically, the acoustic gramophone did not capture the voice of either soprano particularly well. Melba could be scathing about other singers. Interestingly, she appears not have had a high opinion of record- ings of her own voice. She is reputed to have said that if she really sounded as she did on disc, no one would come to hear her. Nevertheless, she made many records and demanded high royalties. Unlike the thriftless Tet, who died in financial straits, Melba was a good business woman and held on to her fortune.*

Although they had sung together in Verdi's *Otello* in 1908 (when McCormack sang the supporting role of Cassio to Melba's Desdemona) their first performance togeth- er as principals was on 30th May 1910 in *La Bohème*, which was also McCormack's debut as Rodolfo. The *Daily Telegraph* reported that he 'acquitted himself remark- ably well, and sang "Che gelida manina" and the rest of the grateful music with real lyrical feeling and beauty of tone'.

During that first season of 1907, McCormack had the opportunity to appear with the Royal Choral Society in Mendelssohn's oratorio *Elijah* at the Royal Albert Hall. However, *The Illustrated London News* of 16th November reported that the tenor 'who has been received with so much enthusiasm at Covent Garden, was hard- ly so successful here, his voice being unable to fill the Albert Hall'. This was one of

Dublin Oratorio Society.

(SIXTH SEASON).

PROGRAMME

OF

HANDEL'S

"Messiah"

Royal University Buildings

(By kind permission of the Senate),

TUESDAY, 22nd DECEMBER, 1908.

SOLOISTS:

Mr. J. F. McCORMACK

Miss AGNES TREACY

Miss MAY DURKIN

Mr. ROBERT RADFORD

Chorus and Orchestra of 250 Performers.

LEADER OF ORCHESTRA - MR. ARTHUR DARLEY.

CONDUCTOR - MR. VINCENT O'BRIEN.

PRICE TWOPENCE.

O'Brien & Ards, Printers, Dublin.

McCormack sang very little oratorio. This appearance with the Dublin Oratorio Society in a performance of Handel's Messiah, conducted by Vincent O'Brien, was one of the few. Note that he is still described as J F McCormack.

the few occasions when the size of his voice was called into question. But there was no doubting the impression McCormack had made in his first year at Covent Garden. Under the heading 'Music in 1907: The Year Reviewed', *The Graphic* noted that, while the instantaneous success of Tetrazzini was the event of the year, there were other notable newcomers: 'Among them being the young Irish tenor, Mr John McCormack, whose success was particularly gratifying, as it is not often that our native artists are enabled to distinguish themselves in leading parts.'

Compared with many singers who struggle in the shadows for years before breaking through to prominence, McCormack had established himself in London in a matter of months, and at Covent Garden in a little over a year since he arrived in the city. When he had watched Enrico Caruso from the gallery of Covent Garden on his honeymoon in July 1906, he had vowed to Lily, 'If I ever get my foot down there it'll take a hell of a lot to get it off.' In the end it took a world war.

Along with his career at the Royal Opera, which carried great prestige, McCormack was also establishing himself as a favourite singer in Edwardian high society and enjoying to the full the charm of the years leading up to the war. Mrs Claude Beddington in *All That I Have Met* evoked those spacious summers:

> In 1907 and 1908 Mr and Mrs McCormack lived at a picturesque, old-world country house, New Copse, in Surrey, and there entertained week-end parties, including great singers like Vanni Marcoux (to my mind the king of diction on the operatic stage), Sammarco and Scotti.
>
> McCormack, always keen about exercise, played a great deal of lawn tennis, also hand-ball, which may be described as the Irish equivalent of fives. Another favourite recreation was 'putting the shot,' a weight of 16lbs.
>
> One of the charms of these week-end house-parties was that all the guests were free to do as they liked. Breakfast began at 10 am; luncheon was missed out, and at 3 pm a sumptuous tea was served – on the lawn in fine weather; dinner, accompanied by the choicest wines (of which John is a real connoisseur) was eaten at 7.30 pm, and then music was made, the like of which had never been heard in the Surrey Hills.
>
> Queen Alexandra was a frequent visitor at Lady de Grey's house at Kingston-on-Thames, and nothing delighted Her Majesty more than to hear McCormack sing on the many informal occasions arranged there by the artistic hostess. In every instance Lady de Grey, with her usual thoughtfulness, sent

her motor to Netherhall Gardens in Hampstead to fetch McCormack and to send him home again. He thus had the honour of singing to Queen Alexander every summer from 1908 to 1914.

Following his success in the Autumn Season of 1907 at Covent Garden, McCormack was engaged there as a *primo tenore* there for the more prestigious Royal Opera, or Summer Season, of 1908. He continued to sing for seven consecutive Summer Seasons, until 1914 when the First World War temporarily closed the house. The only secondary role he ever sang at Covent Garden was that of Cassio in Verdi's *Otello* when Giovanni Zenatello and Leo Slezak took the title role in 1908 and 1909 respectively. There was a strong wing of Italian tenors at Covent Garden in those pre-war days, not only Zenatello and Slezak, but Giuseppe Anselmi, Alessandro Bonci and the great Caruso himself. For an Irish singer to compete among these continental names was quite something. *The Graphic* pointed out wryly:

> If our grandfathers were able to arise from their graves and once more take their places in their old stalls at the opera [and] Covent Garden should ask them to listen to the singing of a… homely John McCormack [it] would seem to them a piece of unbounded impertinence… though they would, no doubt, be ready and willing enough to applaud the efforts of M Max Cormacski, the eminent Polish tenor. [This was a reference to the fabled Polish tenor Jean de Reske (1850–1925) who was a favourite at Covent Garden and indeed wherever he sang.]

Another home-grown tenor making his debut in 1908 was none other than Walter Hyde, he who had taken over from McCormack in Liza Lehmann's opera *The Vicar of Wakefield*. Hyde did not fare so well at Covent Garden, however. Harold Rosenthal, author of *Two Centuries of Opera at Covent Garden* remarked that, as Pinkerton in *Madama Butterfly*, he 'sang with such excellent tone and expression that the result was never in doubt; however, being a beginner and English, he was given little other work during the season'. If to be English was to court prejudice why not also to be Irish? Why was an exception made of McCormack? The answer surely lies in what the *Daily Telegraph* had already said of his Mozart – 'a sense of phrasing that was exquisite'.

Nineteen hundred and eight was something of an *annus mirabilis* for McCormack. At the beginning of the year, under the auspices of Percy Harrison, he made a concert tour of English provinces, as a supporting artist to Emma Albani (1847–1930), the great Canadian soprano who had seen better days both vocally and financially, but was still a name to draw English crowds. In the autumn, he sang at the Birmingham Festival under Henry Wood, appearing in Mendelssohn's *Elijah* again and Verdi's Requiem. The tenor role in the Requiem was hardly suited to his voice and he was not received with much enthusiasm in *Elijah*. When he sang in the oratorio at

Photograph of the violinist Fritz Kreisler inscribed: 'To Mr John McCormack in sincere admiration for the great artist and true friendship for this splendid man. Fritz Kreisler, April 6, 1914.'

the Birmingham Musical Festival again under Henry Wood (who would become Sir Henry Wood in 1911), *The Times* criticised the choir for: '…the prolonged penultimate note of the cadence to the chorus "He, watching over Israel" [that] seemed like a trick caught from Mr McCormack, who did the same at the end of "If with all your hearts".' And the same paper had a harsher criticism for McCormack who 'unfortunately brought the defects of a lower operatic tradition into his singing and especially the tendency to make English words ridiculous by singing the vowels as though they were Italian ones.'

Of more lasting importance to McCormack was a short concert tour he made with Fritz Kreisler (1875–1962) at this time, during which the two men struck up a lasting friendship. McCormack was unequivocal about what this friendship meant to him. In his unpublished memoirs, quoted by Lily in *I Hear You Calling Me*, he wrote:

> Financially it [the tour] was a 'flop', but in every other way it was of inestimable value to me. The kindly advice and the criticism which I received from Fritz in those few concerts had a greater influence on my work than any other thing before or since. A constructive critic in the true sense, he gave me a piece of advice I've never forgotten. He said, 'John, learn the music as the composer wrote it, be absolutely letter perfect, and then put your own interpretation upon it.' No words of mine can add lustre to the

83

name of this great artist. He has always remained my ideal violinist. No one who has not enjoyed his friendship can really estimate the man, as well as the artist.

Concert and oratorio work was secondary to his appearances as a *primo tenore* at the Royal Opera House during the Summer Season when he again sang in *Cavalleria Rusticana* and *Rigoletto* and added the roles of Edgardo in *Lucia di Lammermoor* and Alfredo in *La Traviata*, roles he shared with the one tenor who challenged Caruso's supremacy in the States, Alessandro Bonci.

It was on McCormack's first night of the Summer Season that Caruso went backstage, Lily recalled, to wish her husband luck. 'John was fairly taken off his feet by surprise. He knew that Caruso was not singing that evening and he couldn't imagine the reason for the call. When John asked, "What are *you* doing here this evening?" Caruso replied in Italian, "You don't think I'd let the night pass without wishing you good luck, do you?" I hope that Enrico realised how much this meant to John.' According to the story associated with an autographed picture of Caruso, it was not until two years later, in Boston, that McCormack confessed to Caruso that he had once forged his signature with an inscription to himself. Greatly amused – Lily remembered the Italian tenor's 'booming laughter' – he immediately signed a photograph: 'To McCormack very friendly Enrico Caruso, Boston 1910'. Their friendship was a remarkably warm one.

At the end of May 1908, McCormack had three engagements on consecutive days, any one of which might have seemed unimaginable to him a few years earlier. The old guard loomed large on 26th May when a concert was held at Queen's Hall to celebrate the Diamond Jubilee of conductor Wilhelm Ganz (1833–1914). Here was the English establishment in all its pomp, with a duke, no less than five earls, a viscount and the Speaker of the House lending their names to the organisation of the concert. Ganz had once toured as accompanist to Swedish soprano, Jenny Lind (1820–1887) and he had had a long association with the legendary soprano, Adelina Patti (1843–1919). Lind was but a memory, albeit a revered one; but Patti was still active, and came out of retirement (yet again) to participate in the proceedings. In a review of the 19th-century sopranos entitled 'The Prima Donna as "Musician"', *The Times* concluded that: 'All 19th-century divas had some defect to be overcome save Patti, a singer: "by the grace of God".' It would be difficult to exaggerate the esteem, indeed awe, in which Patti was once held, not only by the public at large, but, more tellingly, by colleagues who recognised her pre-eminence. Among the singers and actors who appeared at the concert, which included tenor Ben Davies, a great favourite in London; soprano Ada Crossley; the Polish bass Edouard de Reske; violinist Mischa Elman; and, from the stage, Irene Vanbrugh Lewis Waller, Charles Hawtrey – Patti was the star. At sixty-five, there was little of her voice left, but that did not seem to matter much to an English public whose usual response to her was that of adulation. Patti had the aura of a queen and was treated as such. She was, declared *The Graphic*: '…the life and soul of the entertainment, singing several times, and afterwards kissing

Photograph of Enrico Caruso inscribed: 'To McCormack very friendly Enrico Caruso, Boston 1910'. Caruso had whipped up this photograph and signed it in response to McCormack confessing to him that he had once forged his signature and signed it to himself!

the hero of the day and crowning him with a laurel wreath.' She sang 'Voi che sapete' and Tosti's 'Serenata' and gave as encores Gounod's 'Serenade', 'Home, Sweet Home' and, from the 18th century, Antonio Lotti's 'Pur dicesti'. In the midst of all this, Ganz accompanied the singers and played Grieg's Violin and Piano Sonata in F.

McCormack got caught up in the excitement of the event and wrote on his programme: 'Most important as was occasion of my only appearance with Patti.' According to Lily, he went out and bought a copy of Patti's recording of 'Pur dicesti'; and then made his own with the quip, 'This will make the sopranos jealous.' In

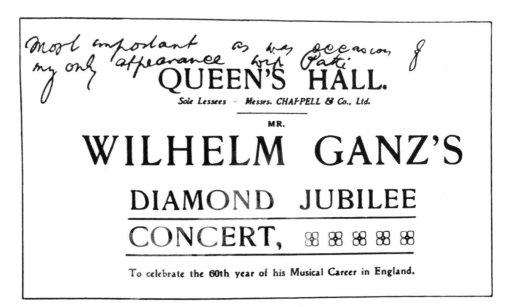

Concert programme celebrating Wilhelm Ganz's sixtieth year in music, with McCormack's note added.

spite of what Lily says, he does not appear to have made a record of 'Pur dicesti' at this time, certainly none was published. He did, however, make a record of 'Pur dicesti' much later, in 1923. This recording is, indeed, a model of its kind: disciplined, with well-judged rhythmic nuances and exemplary trills, each provided with a neat turn. Patti's version, however, has a more infectious sense of fun and spontaneity about it.

The following evening, 27th May, by royal command McCormack appeared in his first gala performance at Covent Garden, held in honour of the President of the French Republic, Armand Fallières. Melba was partnered by Giovanni Zenatello and the French bass Marcel Journet in the second act of Gounod's *Faust*, along with Edna Thornton and Caroline Hatchard. Tetrazzini and McCormack opened the proceedings, with the baritones Mario Sammarco and Vanni Marcoux in the first act of Bizet's *Les Pêcheurs de Perles* – in fact given in Italian as *I Pescatori di Perle*, the

*Adelina Patti
(1843–1919)
perhaps the most
celebrated soprano
of the 19th century.*

convenience of the prima donna taking precedence over the sensibilities of the French president. *The Times* reported on the occasion:

> Some twelve hours before the doors were opened, the more determined of those who had hoped to secure seats had begun to collect, with camp-stools and other means of comfort for their long day of waiting. By eight o'clock, when the doors were opened, the crowd on the pavements of the troop-lined streets was dense, and a large number of police were busily engaged in keeping the approaches clear.

Those lucky enough to gain admission would have seen that the theatre had been decorated with an estimated quarter of a million rose blooms, a proportion of which had to be artificial for fear the ladies might faint. But *The Times* thought that 'no anticipations could do justice to the lightness and grace of those broad bands and rippling festoons of roses which covered all the tiers, beginning with pale pink at the proscenium and shading gradually to the richest Royal crimson opposite the stage'. If roses, by virtue of their number, were the most conspicuous feature in the house,

they were not the most exotic. 'The most brilliant feature... before the arrival of the Royal party,' *The Times* suggested was to be found in 'the two boxes to the left of the grand tier', which were occupied by the Maharajah of Nepal and his suite: 'His Highness was wearing a headdress of incomparable splendour, a helmet composed entirely of diamonds and emeralds, and a bird of paradise and an osprey.' History, rather than headdress, marked out such attendees as H H Asquith, the

Newspaper advertisement for first Gala Performance in which McCormack sang on 27th May 1908, to honour the President of the French Republic, Armand Fallières. French or not, I Pescatori di Perle was given in Italian. McCormack also sang in the Gala to mark the accession to the throne of King George V in 1911.

prime minister; Sir Edward Grey; A J Balfour; and Winston Churchill. *The Times* found the sight in the auditorium almost impossible to describe, for the reason that: 'When all the rank and fashion of England are collected into a comparatively small space and all in costumes worthy of the occasion, it is difficult to convey any impression of the effect on the eye' but it could not forgo picking out Lady Londonderry, 'whose tiara, necklace and stomacher attracted all eyes'.

Accoutrements of gold and crimson hangings, old French furniture, gilt mirrors and quantities of palms were used to decorate the front entrance for the royal party. (Sir John Murray Scott may have played a role in this as he was a friend of King Edward VII.) As word spread that the king had arrived, 'a whisper rang through the house', and 'the King's Indian orderlies were seen to take their places in the stalls'. The directors of the opera syndicate received the king and queen and the French president, and the party was then led by Silver Stick Adjutant-in-Waiting up the stairs, which was lined with a guard of the king's bodyguard of the Yeomen of the Guard. At last the 'Marseillaise' was struck up, followed by the British national anthem and then the performance began with Tetrazzini 'ably supported' by McCormack.

The last of the three engagements took place at the Royal Albert Hall on 28th May, when a concert was given on behalf of the League of Mercy with invitations issued by the Prince and Princess of Wales. The artists included Caruso, Melba, Maria Gay, Ben Davies, the venerable English baritone Charles Santley (the first singer ever to be knighted), Antonio Scotti, the violinist Efrem Zimbalist and the cellist Josef Hollman. The accompanists included Paolo Tosti, Landon Ronald (who was an important figure in the early recording industry) and none other than Hamilton Harty who had accompanied McCormack at the Feis in 1903.

These were heady days for the young tenor. Without the long drawn out apprenticeship that is the lot of so many hopefuls, he had been catapulted into the forefront of the Edwardian musical scene. The threadbare clothes in which he had arrived in London were quickly replaced with an immaculate morning suit, silk hat and fine silk scarf. In such attire, he took to attending rehearsals, with the result that at least one conductor regarded him as 'being too dressed up to be a serious artist'. The conductor could not have been more mistaken. Lily remembered him as a 'glutton for work', relentlessly working on his voice and technique. He had a disciplined approach towards his work. He made a point of not going out the night before a performance and, on the day, developed the habit of speaking, if at all, only in a whisper; quite a sacrifice for a man who was talkative and ebullient by nature.

If he was deadly serious about his work, he could be equally serious about his dignity. Failing to make a rehearsal on time, he was rounded on by Harry Higgins. McCormack apologised but explained that he had not received notification. Higgins rejected the explanation and replied that in future notification would be sent to him for every rehearsal whether he was required or not. McCormack lost his temper and retorted that he would turn up when he got the next notification, but if it turned out he was not required he would not come to any further rehearsals. He then left Higgins' office. There was some anxiety at home after this heated exchange, but Lily did not try – she probably knew better – to persuade her hot-headed husband to back down. In the event, no notification was sent to him when he was not required and nothing further was heard of the matter. However, it could have brought his career at Covent Garden to an abrupt end.

Success meant McCormack was not long satisfied with the little terraced house in Streatham and Lily was expecting another child during the summer of 1908. Long before the two-year lease was up on the Streatham house, they were on the move again. This was a pattern frequently repeated. McCormack needed a helpmate who could put up with being constantly uprooted and on the move. Lily was adaptable, good at providing a home in what, in many ways, was a rootless life. McCormack took a lease on Rosaleen House in Hampstead, a much larger house with a superior address. No longer satisfied with the furniture they had for the Streatham house, he got rid of it and started all over again.

He certainly liked to do things in style. Even before he had left Streatham, St Patrick's Day – or St Patrick's Week as John liked to think of it – was celebrated by the sudden arrival at Streatham Hill of a liveried chauffeur along with a large car. McCormack was earning a great deal more than he had been even six months earlier and he intended to live up to every penny of it. As his earnings increased exponentially, so did his expenditure and this would be the pattern right through his career. 'Strange that the first "words" we had in our married life were because of John's extravagance,' wrote Lily. At this point, 1908, he found himself overstretched financially and made an approach to Sir John Murray Scott who had a rule never to lend money – or so he told McCormack. It was only the look of disappointment on his face that persuaded Sir John to make an exception. A date was set for repayment and McCormack met the deadline. It was made plain that, had he failed to do so, the friendship would have been at an end. So with money in his pocket, the pattern was repeated: while Lily had her confinement for the birth of Gwendoline, who arrived on 21st July 1908, John was once again furnishing a new house himself.

Looking back at his eight seasons at Covent Garden, McCormack's greatest success is usually taken to have been Don Ottavio in *Don Giovanni*. Yet London was ambivalent towards Mozart, and it is worth pointing out that the reviews of McCormack in Mozart's works were not always as enthusiastic as in other operas, some of which today we might think were less suited to his gifts.

'For some inexplicable reason,' wrote the critic of *The Graphic* on 16th November 1907, 'the music of Mozart seems to have fallen into disfavour of late.' Adding that,

'Mr McCormack… sang beautifully but he seems to forget that it is advisable even for an operatic tenor to have some rudimentary knowledge of the art of acting.' On 24th April 1909, *The Illustrated London News* remarked of *Don Giovanni* and *Le Nozze di Figaro* that, 'it is a notorious and unpleasant fact that neither of these delightful works can fill the opera-house'. *The Times* said much the same, opening its review of 8th November 1907 by stating that: 'A performance of the immortal Don at any other moment of an opera season except the last week is a thing almost unknown in London, and it is to be recorded with gratitude that a repetition is announced for next Monday.'

Come 1910, *The Illustrated London News* changed its mind, remarking on 2nd July that: 'Last week was full of surprises. In the first place, London developed a sudden and violent liking for Mozart…' *Don Giovanni* was staged in four of the eight seasons in which McCormack sang: 1907, 1909, 1913 and 1914. In 1909, when the Swedish baritone John Forsell played the Don, *The Times* went no further than to say: 'Mr John McCormack was again the faithful and fatuous lover, and discharged his duties commendably.' The same paper added a, sardonic remark aimed at those who came to the opera to be seen rather than to enjoy the performance: 'There was a large audience, who showed their interest not only by applauding the performers but by listening to the music.' In the 1913 revival, *The Times* thought: 'The most excellent was Mlle [Emmy] Destinn', and that, 'Mr McCormack who was allowed both his arias, sang them well, and no more can be expected of a Don Ottavio.' Praise to be sure, but hardly a rave review; and an interesting use of the word 'allowed'.

By 1914, at which time it might be thought McCormack was reaching the very peak of his powers, *The Times,* in noting that there was a large turnout for the opera, said on 3rd July that: 'One could wish for nothing better than Mlle Destinn's forceful phrasing in the music of Donna Anna, and though it is not possible to say the same of either Mr McCormack or Miss Elsa Stralia, yet the former's easy singing is always pleasant if rather monotonous in quality.' Surprisingly unenthusiastic praise, if praise it can be called.

The Illustrated London News, in reviewing the 1913 revival of *Don Giovanni*, harked back to an earlier performance noting that:

> One can remember the heartfelt disgust of the few when, a few years ago, Caruso appeared as Don Ottavio, and, apparently concluding that the composer's music was not sufficiently orna-mental, added various little flourishes on his own account, to the immense delight of the *profanum vulgus* and the immense indignation of those who are musically pure at heart.

Yet the obvious comparison that might have been made between Caruso, who no one would think suited to the part, and McCormack was not made. Destinn as

Enrico Caruso was famous for his lightning cartoons. This pair, of himself and McCormack, was done on a menu card for the Savoy Hotel. To judge from the Italian's receding hairline, the sketches must have been done in 1913–14, both during Caruso and McCormack's last season at Covent Garden.

Donna Anna was 'a triumph', but the rest of the cast, McCormack included, were dismissed with: 'Others did well, though they failed to achieve distinction.'

Much warmer praise was given to some of McCormack's other roles. As Edgardo in *Lucia di Lammermoor* in 1908, *The Times* lauded Tetrazzini while declaring that: 'It was well worth waiting until the final scene for Mr John McCormack's admirable singing of the famous tenor song.' The same paper thought he sang the role of Elvino in *La Sonnambula* 'uncommonly well'; while, in *Lakmé* he: '…sang the music of Gerald admirably, and gave the lovely "Cantilena" in the third act with such beautiful phrasing and skilfully modulated tone that he too had to repeat a verse. It was one of the best bits of singing of the evening, and his acting here was good enough to make his recovery after his vigorous assassination almost credible.'

McCormack in the role of Edgardo in Donizetti's Lucia di Lammermoor.

Note the word 'almost'. Over the eight seasons that McCormack sang at Covent Garden, his press showed that there was a consistent dichotomy between his singing on the one hand and his stagecraft and acting on the other. On only one occasion did *The Times* praise his acting. This was when he returned as Turiddu in his first Summer Season: 'In the first scene with Santuzza, especially, there is now purpose in all his movements; nothing is casual or uncertain, but every gesture, to the raising of an eyebrow, has its effect.'

In the light of *The Times'* frequent criticism of his acting after 1908, this review can be regarded as an anomaly, most likely a reaction to the sheer awfulness of his demeanour on stage on his first appearance. Move on three years and, on 11th May 1911, *The Times* was writing of his Rudolfo in Puccini's *La Bohème*: 'If he could only… learn to keep his arms still when there is nothing for them to do, one could easily forgive him his lack of dramatic power.' McCormack was later to say that Rudolfo was his favourite part because he could put his hands in his pockets. Evidently he did not put his hands in his pockets often enough. His comment, in any case, does not suggest a performer with much affinity with the stage.

The Illustrated London News summed up the problem on 2nd August 1913, in reviewing his performance with Melba in Gounod's *Romeo et Juliette*: '…from the vocal point of view Mr McCormack's Romeo leaves nothing to be desired; but it is a pity that such a fine singer does not devote to the dramatic side of his art the full measure of attention it deserves and requires.' It would appear he did not have it in him to make the visual side of an opera performance complement his singing. In 1914, his last year at Covent Garden with nine years of operatic experience behind him, *The Illustrated London News* could write of his Don Ottavio, one of his last performances at the Royal Opera: 'Mr McCormack sang very finely, it was a great treat to hear him, but to watch his inconsequent movement and barren gesture was to lose a part of the pleasure that his voice provides.'

But the separation of eye from ear was a frequent requirement of the opera goer in Edwardian days as surely as it is today and there were few opera singers who could match McCormack for his purity of style and the refinement of his singing. It was enough to make him a firm favourite at Covent Garden; though, even as he established himself in London, he was looking further afield.

CHAPTER THREE

A Golden Age of Opera

M cCormack's friendship with the Sicilian baritone Mario Sammarco (1873–1930) was instrumental in his getting a contract to sing at the San Carlo opera house in Naples, which was by far the largest opera house in which he sang in Italy.

It was remarked by more than one critic that McCormack did not have a powerful voice, yet it is noteworthy that at neither the San Carlo nor at the old Metropolitan Opera House (nor the largest of the concert halls in which he sang in his prime) was the audibility of his voice called into question. The reason is not hard to fathom. A McCormack phrase, sung softly or loudly, has an inevitability about it, its direction is clear and unambiguous. If an audience can readily follow a singer, the volume at which he sings is not likely to be an issue.

McCormack sang two roles at the Teatro San Carlo: Alfredo in *La Traviata* on 19th March 1909 and, six days later, the Duke of Mantua in *Rigoletto*. He confessed himself disappointed with the reception he got, although the press was approving. As Alfredo, *Il Mattino* declared that:

> *Il tenore Mac Kormack fece nel suo debutto ottima impressione. Cantò con buoni mezzi vocali e fu cordialmente festeggiato dal pubblico.* [The tenor McCormack made an excellent impression at his debut. He sang with good vocal means and was cordially applauded by the public.]

The auditorium and proscenium arch of the Teatro San Carlo, Naples.

His duke, if it made less of an impression, nevertheless was well enough approved of by the same paper:

> *Mac Kormack che ha insinuanti qualita vocali messe in evidenza in più parti dell'opera Verdiana.* [Having ingratiating vocal talents, McCormack put into relief most of his role in the Verdi opera.]

Against these reviews, it is surprising that he should have been dissatisfied. The audience response was not what McCormack had hoped for, despite hiring a claque for the first and last time in his life. It did not match the kind of enthusiasm he had learnt to expect at Covent Garden. According to what he told Pierre Key, 'I got applause, oh, yes, I got that – from those who recognised singing when they heard it. What I didn't get was an ovation, which was the thing I had desired, above all else.' If London had found that he only made of the Duke of Mantua a 'rather respectable roué', it is not surprising that Naples was not enamoured with his portrayal either.

By way of comparison, Margaret Burke-Sheridan (1889–1958), the Irish soprano and contemporary of McCormack's, was notably successful in both Naples and

*Photograph of
the baritone Mario
Sammarco inscribed:
'Al gentile collega
Sig. G. MacCormac,
in ricordo Mario
Sammarco London
1907.'*

Right & opposite:
Margaret Sheridan (1889–1958) or Burke Sheridan as she also styled herself. (She also referred to herself as 'Maggie from Mayo' as she came from Castlebar in County Mayo.) She was exceptionally good looking, with blonde hair. In addition to a fine, powerful voice, she had considerable gifts as an actor, and was much admired by Toscanini. Her career was short, only ten years, but they were glorious years in which she sang at both La Scala and the Teatro San Carlo as well as Covent Garden. On the right, she is shown here as Desdemona in Verdi's Otello.

Milan. She, too, had been a pupil of Dr Vincent O'Brien and had once appeared at the Rotunda Rooms, Dublin, in March 1908, in a concert in which McCormack headed the bill. Sheridan, in her prime, which lasted barely ten years, had a voice of considerable power and dramatic beauty, and no doubt her blonde hair, peachy skin and good looks stood her in good stead too. The critic Herman Klein, in reviewing the record she made of the Butterfly duet with Aureliano Pertile, declared: 'This is the real thing… The effect of the duet is soul-stirring, thanks also to the fact that "La Sheridan", as they call her in Italy, has never used her naturally fine voice with so much care, judgement and histrionic ardour.' She made a number of complete operatic recordings and was one of the first, in 1926 at Covent Garden, to be recorded in live performance. These recordings reveal a powerful theatrical instinct.

Klein's phrase 'histrionic ardour' is not a phrase that would readily apply to McCormack, not in opera certainly. It would be a mistake, however, to say that McCormack lacked dramatic flair. There are many records in which his sense of drama is compelling: in miniatures such as Dix's 'The Trumpeter' (1915); Rachmaninov's 'To the Children' (1924 among other years), which he unfolds in a heartbreaking way; in the climactic ending he brings to Liza Lehmann's 'Ah Moon of my Delight' (1911) from *In a Persian Garden*, for instance. And there is no lack of drama in his fine recording of the aria from Beethoven's oratorio *Christ on the Mount of Olives*, which comes close to opera in its sense of drama. Yet when we turn to opera, it is the sheer beauty of his singing in, for example, 'Parigi, O Cara' (recorded in 1914 with soprano Lucrezia Bori) that excites our admiration rather than a sense of impending tragedy. Melodrama was not McCormack's strong suit. His instincts were not of the theatre. And while *The Times* could refer to his Elvino in *La Sonnambula* as having been sung with 'fine intensity of feeling', McCormack was not a Latin by temperament or inclination.

Oscar Hammerstein, an impresario of extraordinary energy, flair and courage. With nothing like the same financial resources behind him, he took on the mighty Metropolitan Opera and more than held his own through several seasons.

Lily had no hesitation in stating: 'I think Italian audiences like a more robust voice than John's. Even Puccini, though I know he attended many fine performances of *La Bohème* given by Melba and John, never went out of his way to praise him.' Certainly lack of power would not have been in McCormack's favour among Italian audiences, but possibly of even more significance was the timbre of his voice. Both Stanislaus Joyce, James Joyce's brother, and Walter Legge of HMV who, initially at least, was put off by the timbre, described McCormack as having a 'white voice'. So too, did Herman Klein, raising the issue more than once in his reviews in *Gramophone Magazine*. The legato line McCormack produced was the equal, if not the superior, of any Italian singer of the time, but the voice was not Italianate in timbre. It had a non-secular purity about it, to coin a phrase, rather than being warmly sensuous in an Italian way; and it was certainly not sensual.

At any rate, McCormack found Italy uncongenial to his talents and did not return. Besides, he had America in his sights.

The Manhattan Opera House had been opened on West 34th Street, New York, by Oscar Hammerstein in December 1906 in opposition to the Metropolitan Opera. For a number of years, Hammerstein's success against his much more powerful rival was, in part, due to his mounting novel operas with strong casts made up of singers seemingly tailor-made for their roles. The arrival of Nellie Melba in January 1907 galvanised audiences at the new venue, and she was Hammerstein's star attraction.

Mary Garden in her
most famous role
of Mélisande in
Debussy's opera
Pelléas et Mélisande.
Her fame was not
confined to her voice
or her acting. When
she took the title role
in Thaïs she wore a
flesh-coloured crèpe
de chine which, in
the words of John
Briggs, 'left a piquant
uncertainty of how
much that was
showing was Garden'.

But Melba remained at the Manhattan for just the one season of 1906–07 before returning to the Metropolitan. A soprano was now needed by Hammerstein as a rival to Melba and Tetrazzini took up the challenge and proved equal to it. In addition, Hammerstein had under contract Mary Garden, one of the greatest singing actresses of the age and often compared with Bernhardt; the charismatic Lina Cavalieri

John and Lily as they would have appeared when they returned to America.

who, for what she may have lacked vocally made up for in sex appeal; and such fine singers as Carmen Melis and Mariette Mazarin. McCormack was to appear with them all. Tetrazzini decided she wanted McCormack to partner her at the Manhattan and recommended him to Hammerstein. Her standing in New York can be judged by *Punch's* 1908 quip that:

> On Wall Street such is… the rage for opera and the great singer
> that men converse and carry on their business solely in recita-
> tive.

Tetrazzini reputation carried far beyond the New York Stock Exchange. When she was indisposed and unable to appear with the Manhattan Company in Cincinnati, McCormack and the rest of the company found themselves singing into a half-empty auditorium.

Initially, Hammerstein was reluctant to employ McCormack. He was pitting some big names against the Met stars, Bonci against Caruso (it is hard to believe from this point in time that the diminutive Bonci was ever a rival to Caruso, but this was the case, at least outside New York). Among the lower voices, no one could out sing Titto Ruffo (the 'Caruso of baritones' as he was sometimes called) who was at the Met; but Hammerstein had Maurice Renaud, a great singing actor, and the ever-popular Mario Sammarco. Mary Garden, quite apart from her impact on stage, provided excellent newspaper copy – her outspoken, indeed sometimes outrageous comments, not to mention her colourful private life, were the match of anything the Met had to offer. Among these established names, why would the Manhattan Opera House benefit from a singer unknown to American audiences and Irish at that? But Tetrazzini had her way and then the penny dropped with Hammerstein: imagine the copy to be had from an Irishman singing Italian opera in New York. What could be more novel? Hammerstein liked it to be thought that he signed McCormack at rehearsal at Covent Garden with the remark: 'Don't you think an Irishman singing in Italian opera in New York is a cinch?' That was good publicity, but Hammerstein was being wise after the event. As McCormack recalled in an interview for *Musical Leader* in 1917: 'Hammerstein kicked against my engagement. And this is how he objected: "An Irish tenor in opera? I don't think so…"' It was Tetrazzini who persuaded him. And McCormack hit New York at just the right time.

The city had become fiercely partisan and curious about opera since this upstart of an opera house had had the impertinence to take on the Met. McCormack could draw another component into the fray: the Irish Americans. McCormack took New York to his heart and New Yorkers took the twenty-five year old tenor to theirs. Even before he had sung a note, McCormack had made an impression in the press, his

Mr. John McCormack Makes His American Debut at the Manhattan Despite Indisposition.

PHYSICIAN ALWAYS NEAR

Despite All He Makes an Excellent Impression—Big Welcome for Mme. Tetrazzini and Other Singers.

MANHATTAN OPERA HOUSE.—LA TRA-
VIATA, opera by Giuseppe Verdi.
Violetta.....................Mme. Tetrazzini
Flora Bervoix.............. }
Annina........................ } Miss Severina
Alfredo.............Mr. John McCormack
Germont......................Mr. Sammarco
Gaston......................Mr. Venturini
Baron Duphol...............Mr. Fossetta
Dr. Grenville...............Mr. De Grazia
Marquis D'Obigny.............Mr. Zano
Giuseppe.....................Mr. Pierucci

Indisposition came very nearly upsetting last night's plans for opera at the Manhattan. It was the first performance of "La Traviata," and it was to mark the American debut of a new Irish tenor, Mr. John McCormack, and the re-entry of Mme. Tetrazzini.

For several days Mr. McCormack has been the victim of the most prevalent brand of a New York cold with a strong leaning toward grippe. So serious was his condition that yesterday Mr. Zenatello was sent for, and was reheared in the rôle of Alfredo. But at half-past five yesterday afternoon Mr. McCormack decided to brave it out. His temperature was high and his spirits low, that a physician accompanied him to the opera house and remained in his dressing room except when the tenor was singing—then he stood in the wings and listened.

It was a trying début, and considering everything Mr. McCormack covered himself with honor. He is a broth of a boy. Twenty-seven years old with a robust frame and a pleasant face. The audience liked him from the start.

He has a light, true tenor voice, which he uses with taste and he won his audi-

MR JOHN McCORMACK, AS ALFREDO.
PHOTO. COPYRIGHT 1909 BY E. F. FOLEY.

Mr. and Mrs. Alexander Revell, of Chicago, and Mr. and Mrs. Arthur Hoppock Hearn.

Mrs. Gary wore a gown of black chiffon satin; the bodice finished with silver spangled net; also a necklace of large pearls. Mrs. Revell was in a Louis XV. gown of Callot blue satin, combined with gold embroidered net and covered with paillettes the same shade as the gown. Mrs. Hearn's costume was of delicate mauve satin brocade, veiled with silver spangled net. She wore also a collar and corsage ornament of diamonds.

Mrs. Paul Morton, in deep violet satin, brocaded with gold, with a chaplet of gold leaves in the coiffure, was with Mrs. James Speyer, who wore a gown of white satin brocaded covered with point lace and corsage ornaments of diamonds.

With Mr. and Mrs. Alfred Graham Miles were Miss Betty Collamore, who was in a gown of blue voile over satin of the same shade; Miss Wellington, in white chiffon and rose colored satin; Mr. George C. Boldt and Mr. William Koch.

Mrs. Miles wore a gown of white satin crepe, veiled in old rose point lace, a necklace of pearls and a collar of diamonds.

With Mr. and Mrs. Isaac Guggenheim were Mr. and Mrs. William H. Fletcher and Mr. and Mrs. Louis F. Rothschild, the latter wearing a gown of palest mauve satin and crepe de Chine, also a collar of pearls.

Mrs. Guggenheim wore a striking costume of steel colored satin, the corsage spangled with steel, also a collar of diamonds.

There were also in the audience Mrs.

boyish charm and forthright manner, his reported praise for Caruso, his saying how much he learnt from the Italian tenor and from Marcella Sembrich, delighted and intrigued readers.

Every singer's nightmare is to be ill on the occasion of an important debut and, sure enough, on 10th November 1909, when the Autumn Season at the Manhattan was to open with Tetrazzini, Mario Sammarco and McCormack in *La Traviata*, the tenor had a dose of flu or perhaps his nerves were even worse than usual. Giovanni Zenatello was put on standby. But McCormack got up from his sick bed and went to the theatre determined to do what he could. 'Physician always near', was a sub-heading of *The New York Herald* while describing him as a 'broth of a boy', and adding: 'Despite all he makes an excellent impression.' *The New York Evening Post* declared: 'That McCormack is a decided acquisition to the company is undoubted.' Adding that: 'He is a pure lyric tenor, with a carefully trained voice; pure, clear, even and flexible, and naturally placed. His tones are always true and sympathetic and his *mezza voce* was most effective.' Evidently, even when ill McCormack did not force his voice. *The New York Times* found that: 'His voice has a delightfully sympathetic quality, and his manner of singing is discreet and refined. The voice is not a power-ful one, but should answer all the demands made of a lyric tenor.'

In Tetrazzini – his fairy godmother – McCormack could not have asked for greater support, even if it may not always have been in accord with the dramatic action on stage. *The New York Evening Post* noted: 'At the outset, in addition to his apparent physical suffering, he was palpably nervous, but Madame Tetrazzini came to his rescue by crossing the stage and giving him a gentle pat of encouragement.' She did more. As *The Record* reported: 'That Tetrazzini fully realises his exceptional ability and delights in singing with him is evidenced in the persistent manner in which she insists upon his assuming his burden of the applause. Last night Tetrazzini literally dragged the hero forth.' Five days later, he appeared as Edgardo in *Lucia di Lammermoor* and according to *The New York Times* 'deepened the impression he had made on his first appearance'. *The New York Herald* was of the same view: 'All the pleasant things that have been said of the young Irish singer's voice may be repeated, with emphasis.' By the time he sang his third role, that of Tonio in Donizetti's *La Fille du Régiment* (*La Figlia di Reggimento*) on 22nd November, McCormack had established himself as a firm favourite in New York. He was, said *The New York Times*, 'in splendid voice and proved himself even more of an artist than he has before, by his singing of the music allotted to Tonio'. *The New York Herald* recorded that the famous tenor aria in the second act, '"Per viver vicino a Maria" was so admirably sung as to win some of the warmest applause of the evening. He had to repeat it.' In fact, he would not have had the opportunity to sing the aria at all had not the French baritone Charles Gilibert, who sang the role of Suplice in the same production, possessed a copy of the French edition of the opera. The original Italian version, used by the Manhattan, did not contain Tonio's famous aria. As the opera was given in Italian, McCormack himself put together a translation, which he also used for the record he made of the aria the following year. The poise of the voice in this recording, the effortlessness, the languid manner in which he floats each phrase echoes John F Cone's remark in *Manhattan Opera Company* that the singing of the aria was 'one of the tenor's greatest vocal achievements in grand opera'.

Tetrazzini and McCormack had an evident rapport on stage that went down well. However, he was less successful with some of the other sopranos in the Manhattan Company. Carmen Melis, playing Santuzza in *Cavalleria Rusticana*, thought McCormack, as the faithless Turiddu, too mild in his manner of treating his lover who, at one point in the opera, he has to shove away from him in a fit of temper. Responding to her criticism, McCormack managed to push Melis so forcefully that she ended up sprawling in the wings. She was shaken and limping when she got back on stage but not otherwise hurt. An enormous bouquet of flowers was his contribution towards smoothing ruffled feathers. Mariette Mazarin is not on record as having made any suggestions such as Melis had done, but offered instead the withering comment: 'Monsieur McCormack… if Turiddu was like you, I should never have had to complain to his mother about my unfortunate predicament.' Where McCormack was concerned, the older, mellifluous operas were one thing, full-blooded *verismo* quite another. A stage lover – or stage cad for that matter – McCormack was not.

At times, the indefatigable Hammerstein was producing opera simultaneously in up to four cities, a remarkable achievement by any standards, and his standards were high but resources were often strained. For example, the production of *Lucia di Lammermoor* in Pittsburgh on 20th December 1909 with the Pittsburgh Symphony Orchestra, allowed for only one rehearsal, and that was without the principals.

In Boston, 'the two giants of grand opera locked horns' when the Manhattan Opera Company appeared at the Boston Theater and, at the same time, the Metropolitan Opera performed at the Boston Opera House. Hammerstein had Mary Garden, Tetrazzini, Mariette Mazarin, the fine contralto Gerville-Réache, Renaud and McCormack against which the Met had Caruso, Geraldine Farrar, Emmy Destinn, Joanna Gadski, Louise Homer and Antonio Scotti. In *Lucia di Lammermoor* on 29th March 1910, Tetrazzini, and particularly McCormack, scored a major triumph, *The Boston Post* went so far as to say: 'Not in years has a tenor voice been heard in this city so pleasing and acceptable.' High praise indeed considering that Caruso had sung 'in this city' just two days earlier.

The two companies had already 'locked horns' by giving the same opera in New York on the same evening! This was when Puccini's *La Bohème* was staged at both

McCormack as Edgardo in Lucia di Lammermoor.

Manhattan Opera House
West Thirty-fourth Street, Near Eighth Avenue.

Manhattan Grand Opera Company
SEASON 1909-1910

FOURTH SEASON OF GRAND OPERA
Under the Direction of
MR. OSCAR HAMMERSTEIN.

Saturday Afternoon, January 22, 1910, at 2 o'clock.

BOHEME
(In Italian.)

Opera in Four Acts, by PUCCINI.

MIMI, a Sewing Girl	MME. CARMEN MELIS
MUSETTE, a Grisette	MLLE. TRENTINI
RUDOLPH, a Poet	MR. JOHN McCORMACK
MARCEL, a painter	M. SAMMARCO
COLLINE, a Philosopher	M. LASKIN
SCHAUNARD, a musician	M. GILIBERT
BENOIT, a Landlord	M. DADDI
ALCINDORO, an Old Roue	
PARPIGNOL	M. FRANZINI
CUSTOMS OFFICERS	M. FOSSETTA / M. ZURO

MUSICAL CONDUCTOR ....M. OSCAR ANSELMI
STAGE DIRECTOR............M. JACQUES COINI

Manhattan Opera House
West Thirty-fourth Street, Near Eighth Avenue.

Manhattan Grand Opera Company
SEASON 1909-1910

FOURTH SEASON OF GRAND OPERA
Under the Direction of
MR. OSCAR HAMMERSTEIN.

Saturday Evening, March 26, 1910, at 8 o'clock.

LUCIA DI LAMMERMOOR
(In Italian.)

Opera in Three Acts, by DONIZETTI.

LUCIA	MME. LUISA TETRAZZINI
ALISA	MME. SEVERINA
EDGARDO	MR. JOHN McCORMACK
ASHTON	M. SAMMARCO
ARTURO	M. VENTURINI
RAIMONDO	M. DE GRAZIA
NORMANDO	M. DADDI

MUSICAL CONDUCTOR........M. OSCAR ANSELMI
STAGE DIRECTOR............M. JACQUES COINI

Manhattan Opera House
West Thirty-fourth Street, Near Eighth Avenue.

Manhattan Grand Opera Company
SEASON 1909-1910

FOURTH SEASON OF GRAND OPERA
Under the Direction of
MR. OSCAR HAMMERSTEIN.

Wednesday Evening, March 2, 1910, at 8 o'clock.

Rigoletto
(In Italian.)

Opera in Four Acts, by VERDI.

GILDA	MME. TETRAZZINI
MADDALENA	MISS ALICE GENTLE
GIOVANNA	MLLE. SEVERINA
THE COUNTESS OF CEPRANO	MLLE. JOHNSTON
THE DUKE	MR. JOHN McCORMACK
RIGOLETTO	M. MAURICE RENAUD
SPARAFUCILE	M. VALLIER
MONTERONE	M. DE GRAZIA
MARULLO	M. FOSSETTA
THE COUNT OF CEPRANO	M. NEMO
BORSA	M. VENTURINI
PAGE	MLLE. KEENAN

MUSICAL CONDUCTOR........M. OSCAR ANSELMI
STAGE DIRECTOR............M. JACQUES COINI

Manhattan Opera House
West Thirty-fourth Street, Near Eighth Avenue.

Manhattan Grand Opera Company
SEASON 1909-1910

FOURTH SEASON OF GRAND OPERA
Under the Direction of
MR. OSCAR HAMMERSTEIN.

Monday Evening, March 21, 1910, at 8 o'clock.

LAKME
(In Italian.)

An Opera in Three Acts, by LEO DELIBES.

LAKME	MME. TETRAZZINI
MALIKA, a Slave	MME. DUCHENE
ELLEN, Daughter of the British Governor,	MLLE. TRENTINI
ROSA, Her friend	MLLE. VICARINO
MRS. BENSON, Governess	MME. SEVERINA
GERALD, a British Officer	MR. JOHN McCORMACK
FREDERICK, a British Officer	M. CRABBE
NILIKANTHA, a Brahmin Priest, and father of Lakme	M. HUBERDEAU
HADJI, a Hindoo Slave	M. RUSSO

MUSICAL CONDUCTOR .... M. CARLO NICOSIA
STAGE DIRECTOR .... M. JACQUES COINI

PROGRAMME.

The Daughter of the Regiment

(In Italian.)

Opera in Two Acts, by DONIZETTI.

MARIA, a Vivandiere ....MME. TETRAZZINI
MARQUISE OF BIRKENFELD.....MME. DUCHENE
TONIO, a Peasant ....MR. JOHN McCORMACK
SERGEANT SULPICE ....M. GILIBERT
MAJOR DOMO ....M. NICOLAY

MUSICAL CONDUCTOR.........M. OSCAR ANSELMI
STAGE DIRECTOR .... M. JACQUES COINI

SYNOPSIS OF SCENERY.

ACT I---A typical Tyrolean village scene.

ACT II---Salon in the Chateau of the Marquise of Birkenfeld.

Manhattan Opera House
West Thirty-fourth Street, Near Eighth Avenue.

Manhattan Grand Opera Company.
SEASON 1909-1910

FOURTH SEASON OF GRAND OPERA
Under the Direction of
MR. OSCAR HAMMERSTEIN.

Monday Evening, February 14, 1910, at 8 o'clock.

LA TRAVIATA
(In Italian.)

Opera in Four Acts, by VERDI.

VIOLETTA ....MME. TETRAZZINI
FLORA BERVOIX ....MISS ALICE GENTLE
ANNINA .... MLLE. SEVERINA
ALFREDO ....MR. JOHN McCORMACK
GERMONT, Father of Alfredo.........M. SAMMARCO
GASTON ....M. VENTURINI
BARON DUPHOL ....M. FOSSETTA
DOCTOR GRENVILLE ....M. DE GRAZIA
MARQUIS D'OBIGNY ....M. NEMO
GIUSEPPE ....M. PIERUCCI

MUSICAL CONDUCTOR ....M. OSCAR ANSELMI
STAGE DIRECTOR.............M. JACQUES COINI

III

the Manhattan Opera House and the Metropolitan on 26th January 1910. Lily had a seat to watch John, but a friend, Mr Crimmins:

> …was one of the few people I know who heard *Bohème* in two places on the same night. Hammerstein produced it with the ravishing Lina Cavalieri, Sammarco, and John at the Manhattan, and the Metropolitan gave it with Geraldine Farrar, Caruso and Scotti. Mr Crimmins took seats for both performances and he and his daughters alternated, hearing half at each house. He wanted to compare Caruso and John! The world knows who was the greatest tenor, but for beauty it would have been hard to choose between Geraldine and Cavalieri. When the opera was over at the Manhattan, Hammerstein's only comment was, 'Good work, Mike [referring to McCormack]. And we rang down our curtain six minutes ahead of them.' I should have liked to attend both performances myself, but I could not forsake *my* Rodolfo.'

The high standing of the Manhattan Opera Company was memorably marked when President Taft received the entire company at the White House on 12th January 1910 during the company's visit to Washington. McCormack, extrovert, often boisterous and generally in high spirits, could also be subject to surprising fits of shyness. It has been said that he never entirely shook off a sense of provincialism about himself, despite his international stature. Sometimes it got the better of him. Lily recalled:

> President Taft came to the opera and invited John to lunch with him at the White House the next day… In those days such an invitation was 'a command'. Before that luncheon John suffered a worse attack of nerves than before a concert. It was a men's party and, being extremely shy, he couldn't see how he was going to face it without me. I went with him as far as the White House and we walked twice around it before he got up his courage to go in. However, once there, he had a wonderful time…

A feature of Hammerstein's Manhattan programmes were Sunday evening concerts at which both operatic arias and songs were generally featured. Lily remembered one particular concert which was memorable for several reasons:

> Aunty [Lily's sister, Peggy] came over to hear John's American début, sending the children and nurse to my mother in Dublin…

One night [during a concert] after John had sung the aria from *Lucia*, someone asked for 'The Snowy-Breasted Pearl' as an encore. There was no one who could play it. John suddenly thought of Aunty, who had played it for him many times at home. He went over to the wings and whispered to Mr Hammerstein, who came up to our box himself, and before Aunty realised what was happening she was on the stage at the piano with John humming the first bars of the tune in her ear. The house rose and he had to repeat the whole song. John's amusement at Aunty's surprise at finding herself in the limelight was worth seeing.

This was exactly the kind of thing at which McCormack excelled, radiating a genial and spontaneous warmth and plenty of boyish charm in concert, freed of the burden of trying to adopt a stage role. Hammerstein noticed the difference and recognised from the start the potential he had as a recitalist. And in a few short years, McCormack's operatic appearances would become sporadic as he turned more and more to the concert platform.

Oscar Hammerstein could not hold out indefinitely against the Metropolitan and, on the verge of bankruptcy, he signed an agreement in April 1910 with the Metropolitan Opera board that he would produce no more opera in New York, Philadelphia, Chicago or Boston. The Manhattan Opera Company, McCormack included, now became the Chicago-Philadelphia Opera Company under the control of the Metropolitan Opera. The newly named company would perform

John McCormack and W J Guard (Publicity Director at the Metropolitan Opera) outside the stage door of the opera house.

in Chicago and Philadelphia and other major cities, and make guest appearances at the Met in New York. Thus it was that McCormack made his debut at the Metropolitan Opera House, on 29th November, singing opposite Melba in *La Traviata*. Reviews were mixed. Henry Kreibel of *The New York Times* enthused over his 'delicate phrasing… the feeling and tenderness of his art'. W J Henderson, the critic of *The Sun* dismissed this feeling and tenderness, finding it made for a 'mild and inoffensive Alfredo'.

At the beginning of 1910, McCormack was invited to make test records for the Victor Talking Machine Company. Here was a major opportunity. Victor had enormous marketing clout and, as Caruso had found, recording was extremely lucrative and brought his voice to a public that never got near the Metropolitan Opera house or indeed any other. Like Oscar Hammerstein, Calvin C Child of the Victor Company recognised McCormack's gifts in song and as a recitalist. He approached Victor's affiliated company in London, The Gramophone Company, with which McCormack had recorded six years before, with a view to jointly buying out the tenor's Odeon contract, which still had several years to run. The Gramophone Company vacillated so, apparently, Child went it alone, giving Odeon £2,000 to release the tenor and signing him up to an exclusive contract to run until 1938.

Child's belief in McCormack was well repaid. McCormack became one of the three highest-selling artists in the Victor Red Seal catalogue, a title used to denote celebrity performers. Caruso and the Romanian American soprano Alma Gluck were the other two singers whose record sales surpassed those of all other Victor artists of their time. Marcia Davenport, the daughter of Alma Gluck, describing her mother's appeal in her autobiography *Too Strong for Fantasy*, said precisely what was being said of McCormack: 'I think the basis of this [appeal] was the quality of intimacy in her voice, which in concert made each member of the audience feel she was singing directly to him or her; and which came through on her records in a way that made people consider them personal treasures.' Both McCormack and Gluck (who had sung a few seasons at the Metropolitan Opera) would find the concert hall a more congenial setting for their personalities.

McCormack's first year with Victor, 1910, is generally regarded as marking the first year of his vocal prime that would last for ten or twelve more years. His vocal technique is complete by 1910. The voice floats as if on the tip of the breath, the registers are imperceptibly blended, the vocal line a perfect sequence of unsullied notes, each in its place, as illustrated in his recording of 'Tu che a Dio spiegasti l'ali', Edgardo's lament from Donizetti's *Lucia di Lammermoor*, for example. The purity and the freedom of tone was exemplary.

The record industry spread the fame of singers to an audience far larger than ever frequented the opera house or concert hall and McCormack's association with Victor

From the tenor's Australian tour. The photograph is inscribed: 'To my dear friend Vincent [O'Brien] souvenir of my first Romeo and of my Australian season and kindest regard and wishes for New Year from his sincere friend John McCormack Sydney 1911.' He does not cut a very prepossessing figure as Roméo, not with that wig.

would produce, over his career, many hundreds of records as well as prodigious royalties in record sales. He became a great deal more worldly-wise than the provincial boy in London who had taken work and a few pounds wherever he could find them. A letter, dated 2nd June 1914, to his manager Charles L Wagner, reveals a man who had learnt to take care of himself:

> If you remember I told you that he [Calvin Child] told me that Caruso and [Geraldine] Farrar took no advance royalty. Well, Caruso told me on the boat that he gets $50,000 a year advance, that he has fifty cents on large records and twenty-five on small record[s]. Contrast that with my fifteen cents on large and ten cents on small. Of course I have no one to blame but myself as I made that contract voluntarily but I am anxious to see if they will spring anymore. Candidly I don't think they will. I am writing to Mr Child this mail and will tell him a few things…

It was during a performance at Covent Garden in 1910 that Nellie Melba turned to McCormack and asked him if he would join her as principal tenor in the Melba-Williamson opera tour of Australia the following year. He accepted enthusiastically. The McCormack household was on the move once again and that included Lily, the two children and Aunty. Enforced separations were the downside of his career as far as both John and Lily were concerned, and they kept them to a minimum.

Imperious as Melba may have been, and as used to getting her own way as she was, she had met her match in the young Irish tenor. The Australian tour did nothing to make their relationship more cordial. To McCormack, Melba was autocratic and overbearing. To Melba, McCormack was a brash youngster who did not know his place. It is said that, years later, when McCormack was singing at the Theatre Royal in Dublin, he saw a framed picture of Melba and turned it to the wall. Another version of the story says he insisted it be removed.

For the Australian tour, McCormack was contracted to sing three times a week but, according to John Hetherington in his biography *Melba*: 'After eyeing the packed houses he contrived to find the Australian climate so hard on his voice that his third weekly appearance nearly always became impossible unless he was compensated by an extra fee of £100.' Little wonder that there was little love lost between them. For all that, the tour was an artistic triumph for both Melba and McCormack, and a financial success as well. The Melbourne correspondent of *The Times* went so far as to declare that the tour was: 'The most remarkable event that has yet occurred in Australian music… the houses being packed night after night, though prices were exactly three times those to which Australians were accustomed.'

Opera portrait inscribed: 'To my darling father and mother wishing them a Happy New Year with love from John. The Duke in Rigoletto.' From his Australian tour.

McCormack won Australian hearts from the start, beginning with a gala perform-ance of *La Traviata,* playing Alfredo opposite Melba in the title role. *The Melbourne Herald* on 30th October reported that it had made: '...the acquaintance of a prepos-sessing young lyric tenor. A fresh and flexible voice, particularly rich in the upper reg-ister, used with pleasant ease.' More surprisingly, the same paper found that, as the Duke of Mantua in Verdi's *Rigoletto,* McCormack's 'appearance and voice fully vindicated his claim to the position of a ducal lady-killer'. In his appearance perhaps, for he was a good-looking man, but surely not in his acting. More predictable was *The New York Herald*'s comment after he appeared in the title role of Gounod's *Faust* that: 'Into the puppet Faust, Mr McCormack failed to infuse any individuality.' And that: 'His nasal pronunciation of French was not to the advantage of his fine voice.' Nasality is a comment sometimes made against McCormack, not so much by the press as by listeners who do not like the timbre. In fact, he did not produce his voice exceptionally high in the mask.

It is safe to conclude that Melba would never have chosen McCormack as her leading tenor if she had felt he could out sing her. (It is on record that Melba had prevented Tito Ruffo from singing the role of Rigoletto, saying that he was too young to be her father, but it is generally agreed that it was on account of the excep-tional size of his voice, 'a miracle' of sound was how his colleague Giuseppe de Luca described it. At a much later date, when the soprano and baritone's path crossed again, Ruffo is said to have declared that she was now too old to be his daughter! A good story but almost certainly apocryphal.) McCormack's voice had none of that kind of power but, in terms of immaculate phrasing and intonation, his singing was ideally suited to Melba's brilliant vocalism. 'The consonance of the two beautiful voices' was, not surprisingly, the virtue *The Melbourne Herald* alighted upon.

McCormack returned to Australia two years later, in 1913, for a concert tour, and his association with Melba was a useful component for his own burgeoning reputation.

In 1911, a major event took place in America in which McCormack played a part. That rarity, an all-American opera, was mounted by the Chicago-Philadel-phia Opera Company, receiving its premiere in Philadelphia on 25th February and then transferring to the Metropolitan Opera three days later, for three performances. The opera was *Natoma,* the story of an American Indian girl, with music by Victor Herbert to a libretto by J D Redding. McCormack sang the tenor lead of Lieutenant Paul Merrill opposite Mary Garden's Natoma. Redding was American and Herbert, although born in Ireland and educated in Germany, had spent twenty years or so in America. So this opera was regarded as American and thus created a great deal of expectation. Too much as it turned out. Not for the first time, or the last, the ques-tion of production costs intruded. The lavish expenditure was not matched by artis-tic achievement. The American correspondent of *The Times* wailed:

McCormack in the role of Lieutenant Paul Merrill in Victor Herbert's Natoma. *The first of two world premieres in which he appeared.*

Portrait of the composer Victor Herbert, inscribed at the top: 'To my dear friends Mr and Mrs John McCormack with all good wishes Victor Herbert April 1911.' On the bottom he adds: 'And special thanks to you dear John for your fine Paul and your never ending enthusiasm...'

We are a wealthy nation, and when we set out to do a thing we do not spare expense. No expense has been spared in the production of *Natoma* in orchestra, singers, setting, or advertising. The only drawback to the brilliancy of the occasion was that scarcely a gleam of genuine art, of the art that is playful in spirit and indifferent to its wage, had gone into the making of the work.

Consequently, there was nothing to lift the audience from an enthusiasm which was after all only amiable and patriotic to the plane of genuine artistic emotion. That, unfortunately, cannot be tonight. Shall we ever be really musical until we give up trying to buy it?

Composer and librettist had had high hopes for their work. Victor Herbert had told *The New York Times* that his 'whole conception of opera is that it should be based on melody'. But, unfortunately, nothing in *Natoma* was memorable and the libretto came in for particular criticism. Redding had declared that: 'We want to show that an opera can be sung in English', but H E Kreibel dismissed the lyrics as the 'merest doggerel'. Doggerel or not, they were by no means easy to sing. *The Times* critic thought that: 'Several of the principals, notably Mr John McCormack, Mr Mario Sammarco, Miss Lillian Grenville and, somewhat less markedly, Miss Mary Garden, in the title role, might as well have been singing in Italian.' This was one of the few occasions when McCormack's diction was called into question. Mary Garden did have the advantage of having the role written for her and she entered into it as fully as she could. 'She has sacrificed remorselessly, everything to the make-up of the Indian,' observed *The New York Times*, 'and in mask and coiffure, as well as in costume, she has put herself entirely into the character.' This kind of thing was entirely beyond McCormack. *The New York Times* thought that he 'sings the music of the American naval officer admirably and he makes an earnest effort to embody the part, in which his lack of dramatic temperament and skill stands somewhat in his way'. That was a nice way of putting it. Irving Kolodin in *The Story of the Metropolitan Opera* suggested that 'McCormack's Lieutenant Paul Merrill was not merely as bad as the role: it was worse'. The role in which McCormack was most successful in America was that of Don Ottavio in Mozart's *Don Giovanni*. It does not require much characterisation – Don Ottavio is a somewhat colourless figure – but the demands on vocal style are acute. The opera was never staged at the Metropolitan during McCormack's operatic years because, in the words of John Dizikes, 'between 1910 and 1940, the Metropolitan Opera specialised in neglecting Mozart'. It had been put on in 1908, two years before McCormack's Metropolitan debut, with a cast that included Emma Eames, Joanna Gadski, Marcella Sembrich, Antonio Scotti, Alessandro Bonci and Chaliapin – an extraordinary cast list of superluminaries. It was not revived again until 1935, when Ezio Pinza took the title role with Rosa Ponselle as Donna Anna and Dino Borgioli as Don Ottavio. The Met therefore never heard McCormack in any Mozart production though he was arguably the greatest Mozartian singer of his time. The only time he sang Mozart at the Metropolitan Opera was in a concert on 5th April 1914, shared with Maria Duchêne and Neida Humphrey, when he sang 'Il mio tesoro' from *Don Giovanni*, along with three Irish songs, 'The Fanaid Grove', 'The Next Market Day' and 'The Snowy-Breasted Pearl'.

Instead it was in Boston, during the 1911–12 season that McCormack was to have one of the greatest triumphs of his operatic career. The conductor, Felix Weingartner had arrived 'like a thunderbolt into Boston's consciousness' said the *Boston Evening Transcript*; and the highlight of the season was *Don Giovanni*'. The Metropolitan claimed, rather lamely, that a suitable cast could not be mustered for the opera. Boston put forward an outstanding cast consisting of Vanni Marcoux as the Don, Emmy Destinn as Donna Anna, Alice Nielsen as Zerlina, Amada Didur as Leporello and McCormack as Don Ottavio. It was one of those evenings, so rare in opera, when everything seems to come together. In the words of John Dizikes in *Opera in America: A Cultural History*. 'The conducting was supple, energetic but restrained. The sets [by Joseph Urban] glowed with color, vibrant as the performance, cleverly conceived to bring the action close to the audience while not impeding its quicksilver movement.' It was McCormack's evening. When he had sung 'Il mio tesoro', Weingartner laid down his baton and led the applause.

If fate had so decreed, McCormack might also have sung the role of Don Ottavio in Salzburg at the invitation of the formidable German soprano Lili Lehmann (1848–1929). She was a woman who knew her singing. A leading light at the Salzburg Mozarteum, her repertoire ranged from coloratura parts to Wagner and she is said to have had sung 170 roles. For a production of *Don Giovanni* at the Mozarteum staged in 1914, she planned a cast that included herself as Donna Anna, Mary Garden as Zerlina, Andrés De Segurola as the Don and McCormack as Don Ottavio. McCormack crossed to Europe to take part in the production, got as far as Belgium, heard of the outbreak of the First World War and returned to the States. It was a bitter disappointment. He regarded the invitation as a signal honour and the opportunity never arose again. Two years earlier, he might also have appeared in Russia at the Imperial Opera in St Petersburg had the dates not clashed with other commitments. For the same reason, he could not accept invitations to sing in Buenos Aires, Argentina, in and around 1915, as he was committed to the Royal Opera, Covent Garden.

McCormack said that, if he was to be judged by only one recording, it should be his 1916 version of 'Il mio tesoro' from *Don Giovanni*. It is justly famous. The intonation is exemplary, the voice absolutely centred on the note. The coloratura runs are made with complete accuracy and the vocal line is free of any bluster or fudge. For all that the technique is immaculate, the singing still comes across as utterly spontaneous. If these virtues were not sufficient in themselves, what sets the record apart from any other, is the *architecture* of McCormack's phrasing; the manner in which the voice rises and descends in perfect symmetry. No other recording of the aria equals it.

During the teens of the new century, McCormack's operatic appearances became increasingly less frequent as he devoted proportionately more time to concert tours. After the 1911–12 season at the Metropolitan, he did not sing there again in opera until the 1917–18 season, when he sang the roles of Rudolfo in *La Bohème*, to the Mimis of Frances Alda and May Peterson; Cavaradossi in *Tosca*, opposite Geraldine Farrar, and Pinkerton in *Madama Butterfly*, again with Farrar in the title role. The following season, he sang just Pinkerton in what was his last season at the Metropolitan.

His performance as Rudolfo divided opinion with praise of his musicianship alongside the inevitable criticism of his acting. *The New York Times* thought Rudolfo was 'not one best adapted for him. It needs a livelier dramatic temperament than his,

Metropolitan Opera programme of 20th February 1918 for Tosca *with Geraldine Farrar in the title role and McCormack as Mario Cavaradossi.*

*McCormack in
the role of Mario
Cavaradossi in
Puccini's opera
Tosca.*

a potency of more passionate expression', although the paper recognised that his singing was 'of its kind unsurpassable, in quality of tone, in purity of diction, in finish of phrase...' *The Sun* thought his singing 'excellently suited' to the role of Rudolfo; but found that in *Madama Butterfly* he was 'inconceivable as a whale-boat officer', while recognising that he sang the music 'surpassingly well'. He was Cavaradossi to Geraldine Farrar's *Tosca* on 20th February 1918, which drew the predictable comment from *The New York Herald* that: 'Dramatically, Mr McCormack is not an ideal Mario [Cavaradossi]', nevertheless *The New York Herald* reported that he: '...earned an ovation after Cavaradassi's air in the closing act, which he sang quietly seated at the prisoner's table. The Irish tenor has not been in better form in any opera, either during his occasional Metropolitan appearances this season, or years ago at the Manhattan.' It was a fitting review for what was his last appearance at the Metropolitan.

By 1918, when he was at the height of his vocal powers, McCormack's career and reputation were centred on the concert hall.

CHAPTER FOUR

Fame, Fortune and a New Career

Forthright in all things, McCormack had no difficulty in admitting that he was a poor actor, the implication being that opera was not therefore his true métier. But indifferent acting on the opera stage is the rule rather than the exception. Why should it have mattered so much in McCormack's case?

He said that his acting was no better or no worse than Melba's. She was known to take up a position centre stage, or at the front of the stage, and let fly with her magnificent voice. Acting was very much a secondary consideration. The illusion of a wasting consumptive must have been less than overwhelming when Tetrazzini sang the role of Violetta in *La Traviata* or Mimi in *La Bohème*. She was a roly-poly woman of some considerable weight and very short indeed. No matter, it was the thrilling vocalism that counted. She *did* have a sense of drama, but was not averse to stepping out of the role from time to time as the mood took her.

Writing of her first performance in *La Traviata* at the Manhattan in 1909, *The New York Times* noted that 'she threw a kiss to the audience as she entered'. If she spotted someone in the audience she recognised, Tetrazzini was apt to acknowledge them with a wave or a wink. Not surprisingly, the same paper felt obliged to add that: 'Much that she does cannot meet with serious approval.' We have seen how, at McCormack's debut at the Manhattan, she crossed the stage to give him a pat of encouragement. Never mind the requirements of the drama nor the disapproval of the critics, the audience loved her and roared their approval. The opera, when Tetrazzini was singing, would appear to have had elements of cabaret about it, with moments of drama added. It is doubtful if she ever remained in a role for a whole performance. In 1911, when she sang in *La Sonnambula, The Times* summed up her performance tactfully with the comment that: 'In spite of many circumstances which make it difficult to regard Mme Tetrazzini as an ideal representative of the anaemic and neurotic Amina, the music suits her so well...'

Realism was certainly not a preoccupation of stage productions at the time when McCormack was appearing in opera and anachronisms abounded. When Tetrazzini appeared as Violetta at Covent Garden in 1910, *The Times*, on 25th April, said: 'It is hoped that if the part is Violetta again she will find time to look in the wardrobe for Violetta's costume, which could hardly have been dated, as hers was, sixty years later than Alfredo's.' The hope was in vain for, when the opera was played the following year, the same paper, on 6th May 1911 noted that: 'The style of the costumes covered a wide range from the crinoline period to that of about 1908; as an illustration of the determination of taste in fashionable circles the contrast was not without value.' Things were no different when she appeared at the Manhattan in New York:

> ...the costuming of this opera has always been a matter of doubt. There are some in Tetrazzini's audiences who wait with bated breath for the rise of the curtain to see what period is to be graced by the story of Violetta's unfortunate history. For years, the chorus and all but the leading soprano wore costumes of the eighteenth century, while she wore a gown of the latest mode.

It was the same at the Metropolitan Opera in November 1909 when *The New York Times* noted: 'Madame Melba wore her 1830 gowns, and the rest of the cast reverted to eighteenth century garb.'

In the present day, it is not often that the opera represents a unified dramatic illusion and it probably happened less often then. Very often it was not even attempted. The *Aida* presented at Covent Garden on 23rd October 1907, with Felia Litvinne as Aida and Mario Sammarco as Amonasro, had the baritone doing his duty by the role and blackening up while Litvinne did not, an inconsistency that did not go unremarked: 'Her complexion was far too many shades lighter than that of her dusky Ethiopian papa,' commented *Punch* magazine, while *The Graphic*, tongue in cheek, suggested that no one:

> ...could possibly have taken her for the daughter of that splendid artist, Sig. Sammarco, for Amonasro's complexion was aggressive-ly Ethiopian, while that of Aida was of the tint known to *modistes* as pale biscuit. Perhaps, however, Mme Litvinne has unearthed

some interesting record of the part which proves Aida's mother
was an albino.

When he first took the role of Otello at Covent Garden, Giovanni Zenatello did no
better. In a review dated 11th July 1908, *The Illustrated London News* found that he

TEMPORARY MISUNDERSTANDING IN AN ETHIOPIAN
FAMILY.

Aïda . . Mme. Litvinne.
Amonasro . Sig. Sammarco.

*Cartoon of Mario Sammarco as a thoroughly black Amonasro and Felia Litvinne as his rather fairer
daughter Aida from* Punch *magazine (23rd October 1907).*

Nellie Melba as
Desdemona.

Luisa Tetrazzini, who had a spaghetti dish named after her, did not look much like a consumptive wasting away.

'does not look the part'. The same journal dismissed Melba with the comment that she 'was never Desdemona for five minutes on end', but as the *Daily Telegraph* found her 'infinitely more convincing than is sometimes the case', it is a matter of wonder how bad her acting could be.

In this milieu, why should McCormack's lack of acting ability and the fact that he had, as *The Times* observed on 11th June 1913, 'the same gestures to suit all occasions' have mattered?

It mattered because the term 'acting' can mean something other than characterisation and adoption of a role. In terms of portraying a character, it may well have been true that McCormack was no better and no worse than Nellie Melba. But a stage performer may convince an audience by strength of personality irrespective of characterisation. Melba was a figure of authority on stage, knew how to fill it, and had a regal and fashionable deportment, all of which her audience could readily respond to, even if she was not Desdemona 'for five minutes on end'. Tetrazzini was hardly regal, but she knew how to engage with an audience, her vivacity, her *joie de vivre*, her love of an audience and not only her spectacular way with her voice, won hearts. As Tet herself said in an interview with the *Daily Express* on 10th March 1929, entitled 'Tetrazzini gives a singing lesson':

> The first thing in singing is, of course, a good voice; the second is wise training; but the last has really nothing to do with voice production. Yet it is the most important of all – Personality. You may have the voice of an angel, and have it trained by a maestro

who is a demi-god, but unless you are gifted with a personality which gives equal pleasure to your audience, you will never become popular or famous... Naturally, I have always taken care to put personality into my work.

McCormack's problem was that his instincts were not theatrical. A stage role, any stage role, inhibited him. He felt awkward on stage and it showed. The one role he could play was himself, when he was not fettered by theatrical costumes and all the stage business and interactions that opera requires. It was by himself, as himself, that McCormack could hold an audience in the palm of his hand as hardly another singer could. It was often remarked by those who had attended a McCormack concert that they came away with the curious experience that he had sung to them personally. He was relaxed on the concert platform in a way he never was in opera, with a warmth and a boyish charm.

Stage performers very often feel secure behind a mask, and vulnerable without one. By way of comparison, Enrico Caruso was a theatre performer rather than a concert platform singer; in this respect he was the very opposite in terms of inclination to McCormack. In his autobiography, *Seeing Stars*, the concert agent Charles L Wagner provided a somewhat mischievous portrait of Caruso as a recitalist. As Wagner acted for McCormack and not Caruso, as no doubt he would have liked to have done, this perhaps needs to be borne in mind in regard to what he wrote. Nevertheless, that Caruso was ill at ease on the concert platform has been well attested to:

> Caruso, for all his greatness on the operatic stage, was not a recitalist... One day I mentioned concerts and it startled him.
>
> 'Never!' he cried. 'I am for the opera – in costume I am in character and comfortable – in a dress suit – what would I do with my hands?'
>
> When, several years later, Coppicus [F G Coppicus, founder of the Metropolitan Musical Bureau] offered him double and triple fees, like a good foreigner he soon found out what to do with his hands – he held them out!
>
> Caruso always was ill at ease on the concert platform. He would take a dozen songs to the piano on each appearance scheduled on the program. After each one, he would look around, measure the distance to the wings, and then sing another song. He seemed to be worried as to how to get on and off stage. Many times he would sing six or eight songs to a group, so as to obviate the necessity of making those dreaded entrances and exits.

John and Lily with their two children, Cyril and Gwen.

What McCormack could do on the concert platform was immediately evident when he arrived in the States in 1909. The first American concert in which he took part, at the Manhattan Opera House on 18th November 1909, proved a great personal success. Hammerstein immediately advertised his next concert for 11th December with the tenor given top billing, and no less significant was the bracketed announcement after his name that: 'He will sing "The Snowy-Breasted Pearl".' The die was being cast as to McCormack's future direction. *The New York Herald* on 13th December commented:

Of the singers, Mr John McCormack pleased the audience greatly with his Irish ballads, as he had done previously in the same place. Of course, he had to add to the programme in response to the plaudits.

There was no question that it was be the Irish ballads that most people would want to hear. When he was the principal soloist at a Metropolitan Opera concert in 1914, in front of a packed house which it might be expected would have a preponderance of opera aficionados, *The New York Herald* on 6th April 1914 put up the heading: 'Mr McCormack's Irish songs please throng in Opera House', and then made no more than a passing reference to the fact that he also sang Mozart! 'As usual most of his songs were those of his native land, although he first sang an aria ['Il mio tesoro'] from Mozart's *Don Giovanni.*'

The sensational concert career that was about to open up for McCormack needed the marketing clout of a major record company and the support of an energetic concert agency. Things had fallen into place in London with minimal passage of time and they did so in America too. We have seen how he was taken up by the Victor Recording Company with the minimum of delay, even though HMV (still known as the Gramophone Company), Victor's sister company in England, was hesitant to participate in the McCormack deal. It could boast an impressive list of continental tenors, which included Caruso, Leo Slezak, Francesco Tamagno and Fernando de Lucia, and they had besides a list of English oper-

Charles L Wagner who was the tenor's manager in America from 1912 until the early 1920s.

atic tenors. McCormack's potential as a singer of songs for a public that would never enter an opera house – a public far larger than the opera attendees and growing – simply did not rank with them. The brogue may have had something to do with it. Perhaps it was thought that the English public would be put off by it, or they may equally have thought the Irish public was too small and too poor to be worth catering for. It is easy to overlook the fact that the recording industry was not yet the mass-market industry it would become. Disc recordings were expensive: at the top of the pile, a one-sided disc of Melba's cost one guinea at a time when an advertisement for a live-in children's maid might offer a salary of no more than £20–22 a year with 'washing found, no beer'.

Initially, McCormack's concert work was handled by the Wolfsohn Bureau, which was associated with the Chicago-Philadelphia Opera Company. He was not free to change allegiance until he had completed a concert tour in the spring of 1912. He then signed with Charles L Wagner who was confident he could make McCormack a concert sensation and was prepared to invest his own money heavily, both in providing the tenor with advances and in the booking of venues. The role Wagner ascribed to himself, from time to time, in McCormack's rise to fame did not necessarily lose anything in the telling; but there is little doubt that his business acumen was to McCormack's benefit.

Wagner recorded his relationship with McCormack in a chapter of *Seeing Stars* – aptly entitled 'Cashing high notes into bank notes' – and recalled with disapproval how McCormack had been handled by the Wolfsohn Bureau:

> He had been badly managed, both as to his concert appearances under the opera contract and under this farmed-out management. In the first case, on one tour he was sent out with five other singers, all more or less known in grand opera and called the International Company. McCormack himself, who was outstanding in the group, was not properly exploited.
>
> These early managers emphasised his nationality – an unnecessary tactic. John McCormack never belonged solely to the Irish race; he belonged to the entire musical world... During the 34-date Wolfsohn-Quinlan tour, they announced him with green ink and heralded an *Irish ballad singer*. I came to the conclusion when I noted these manoeuvers that shamrocks were no more necessary in exploiting McCormack than carving a polar bear on an ice pitcher...
>
> I stayed with John most of the time he was making the Wolfsohn-Quinlan tour so was able to gauge the effects of these improper managerial moves...

The young recitalist with Vincent O'Brien at the piano during their sixty-two date tour of Australia in 1913. Note the seats on stage grouped around the piano and the singer. Such was the demand for tickets, this became the norm at McCormack's concerts for many years. One fan commented that he would prefer to look at the back of John McCormack than the face of any other singer! McCormack would turn round and sing at least one number to those on stage.

> Business was only fair *en tour*. It looked as though the local managers felt this tenor was good for only one appearance, but I was sure I knew better; that the poor houses were caused by poor management. I had reason to make these close studies of my golden-voice artist. My entire fortune was tied up in his fortune…

Wagner's point was well made. It was for McCormack's singing of Irish ballads – and Irish-type ballads – that many in the audience came to hear him, and these songs extended his popularity far beyond the more-limited catchment of those interested in classical music. But it was one thing to be advertised as an 'Irish ballad singer', with the limitations that would imply, quite another to be presented as a classically trained singer, with an operatic background, whose repertoire included ballads. In the forging of McCormack's reputation in the States, Wagner played an important and energetic role. As he wrote in *Seeing Stars*:

> Always I have contended that it is not solely the artist who draws. The exploitation of his artistry is equally as important. Americans are so busy that they need to be reminded again and again. Even when our houses sold out, our advertising continued, for everyone turned away at the box office probably told a dozen friends that that was the *one* thing he had wanted to hear all season. The public always craves that which is hard to get.

And for that craving Wagner was well repaid. On the strength of only the second tour he organised for McCormack (when 'thank Heaven it was before we had the income tax'), Wagner bought himself 300 acres of land and a colonial house on the foothills of the Berkshires. He remodelled it and called it Dapplemere Farm, an allusion to the first play Wagner had produced called *The Money Moon*. Dapplemere Farm was also known as 'the house that John built'. With all those acres, Wagner caught the farming bug and lost a lot of money on the enterprise. He was not the only one:

> McCormack made all manner of fun of me and farming activities but a few years later the farm bug bit him too. He bought a large place near Darien, Connecticut [he called it Lilydale, it is now the Ox Ridge Hunt Club]. Like everything else John does, it was done well. So was he. He bought a herd second to none and built barns and silos de luxe. Every cow had a stall that would shame a Metropolitan dressing room. They were all treated like artists, while the spell was on. But when the war ceased, so did John's rural activities. He never revealed how much it cost him; neither did I. Some things are too sacred to mention.

That first season, starting in the fall of 1912 with Charles L Wagner, McCormack sang sixty-seven concerts, against twelve appearances in opera. His reputation as a recitalist quickly overshadowed his operatic career. Between 1914 and 1918, he appeared in only nine opera performances in America and none after that. As far as Wagner was concerned, it was as a recitalist that McCormack was to be promoted. However, when the soprano Amelita Galli-Curci, who Wagner was also managing, expressed an interest in singing with McCormack, it was arranged for them to appear together in Chicago in *La Bohème* on 1st December 1918. She had taken Chicago by storm just a couple of years earlier and they got a triumphant reception. Wagner recalls in *Seeing Stars* that:

> Mary Garden occupied her usual stage box, wearing a stunning and costly set of furs. Applauding enthusiastically, she dropped them over the side of the box into the orchestra. Their loss wasn't noticed until she was ready to leave the theater and they were never found. 'That operatic stunt of yours cost me $10,000,' she protested.

When McCormack appeared at the Metropolitan Opera House on 4th February 1918 in *Madama Butterfly* with Geraldine Farrar (daughter of an Irish American base-ball player) and Antonio Scotti, *The New York Times* reported that Galli-Curci:

> [waving] an ostrich feather fan of vivid emerald green, appropriate to the greatest cast the Emerald Isle ever furnished an opera in New York, was a distinguished spectator last night at the Met, where she and her husband occupied orchestra chairs well back on the north side of the house, and at times divided attention with the stars on the stage.

McCormack's appearance on 26th December 1918, again singing the role of Pinkerton, in *Madama Butterfly*, was his last appearance at the Metropolitan Opera.

McCormack and Wagner set gruelling concert schedules that were to take him the length and breadth of the States, to Canada and overseas, helping his fame and popularity grow exponentially. With no air travel, cities could only be reached by rail, road and sea and, by any standards, it was a strenuous regime. Just how strenuous may be judged from a diary Lily kept of McCormack's first concert tour in 1912, of which this is an extract:

> MARCH 6TH: Arrived Denver. Snow and sunshine. John bought new overcoat. Letters from home at last. Good news of all. One letter from Russia asking John to sing in opera there.

> MARCH 7TH: Left after concert for Omaha.

March 8th: Arrived Omaha 4 pm. Had tea and dressed for concert. Leaving for Chicago at midnight. (Train four hours late. Spencer [Spencer Clay, McCormack's accompanist at the time] and I made snowballs outside station to keep warm. John sat in waiting room almost frozen.)

March 9th: Arrived Chicago four hours late. All dead tired.

March 10th: Left after concert for St Louis.

March 11th: Concert tonight. Back to Chicago midnight train.

March 12th: Arrived Blackstone Hotel. John bought me heavenly set of chinchillas – muff and stole. Leave early tomorrow morning for Kansas City.

March 15th: Concert 4 o'clock. Leave 7:30 train for Chicago.

March 17th: St Patrick's Day. Mass 11 o'clock. Concert great success.

March 18th: Arrived Detroit around 4. John got gorgeous floral harp at concert.

March 19th: Left by 12 o'clock train for Columbus. Had tea and dressed for concert.

March 20th: Left 12:15 train for Cincinnati. Had tea and dressed for concert.

March 21st: Left for Cleveland. Got there just in time for concert.

March 22nd: Left at 11.30 for Buffalo. Concert great success.

And so on; and this was one of McCormack's shorter tours, sixty-seven concerts in all. For many years, McCormack continued to sing three times, often more, in a week. No singer today would be likely to attempt such a schedule.

Lily now found that the life she had to led as a concert singer's wife was quite different to the one she had lead when her husband was an opera singer, especially when John's career had been centred around Covent Garden and London. Then, they were together in one place for a reasonable length of time at one stretch; now, he was constantly 'on the road'. But Lily knew what was required:

> From the start my problem was to keep our personal schedule subordinate to the demands of John's professional life... We soon decided that the travelling was too hard for me, so far the most part I stayed in New York with the children unless the concerts were as near as Boston, Philadelphia, or Washington, with a few special trips to Chicago.

When Spencer Clay, McCormack's accompanist went to London to teach, his place was taken by Edwin 'Teddy' Schneider. Wagner had arranged the introduction at the Blackstone Hotel in Chicago, where Schneider was running through songs with the baritone Clarence Whitehill. Always quick to make up his mind, McCormack told Wagner straightaway that he wanted Schneider. 'One of the best things Charlie Wagner ever did for John was to bring him and Teddy Schneider together,' recorded Lily, '...he is as close to us as if he were one of the family.' Schneider, ten years McCormack's senior, was quiet and self-effacing by nature – an excellent foil to the highly strung singer. The partnership lasted twenty-seven years, until Schneider's retirement. Schneider, who was German speaking, played a part in the tenor's study of German *lieder* and shared his interest in searching for both new and old music to sing. Lily wrote: 'I never saw two artists work so unfailingly hard. They would start at the piano right after breakfast and in bad weather would stay there for the entire day, paying no attention to meals.'

Wagner commented in *Seeing Stars*: '[Schneider] remained with John throughout his entire career, and most of the time, I fear, was a rather poorly paid accompanist considering the worth of his contribution and his capacity for work. Singers are seldom generous to assistant artists.' These sentiments Wagner put in a letter to his then assistant manager, Denis F McSweeney who, evidently, relayed them to McCormack. The singer smarted under the criticism, and in a long letter to Wagner from the Hotel Statler, Cleveland, on 13th November 1921, gave a sharp answer. The letter, mainly concerned with management matters and ill-chosen concert venues, is mockingly written in the third person as a riposte to a previous communication in which Wagner has told McCormack to 'drop personalities':

> Mr McCormack further desires to call attention with very deep respect to a remark in a letter from Mr Wagner to his distinguished associate Mr MacSweeney anent the salary paid by Mr

McCormack to his compay [accompanist]. The remark is the comparison between the salary paid to Mr Schneider and paid to Frank La Forge by some person or persons unknown and by one Madame Alda to her accompanist. Mr McCormack in the first place would most respectfully ask Mr Wagner to mind his own damn business and rather more consider the length of Mr Schneider's engagement and that he does not play solos which enforce the engaging of assistant artists by Mr Cormack which in the case of Mr L Forge is avoided. Mr McCormack would with deep respect remind Mr Wagner that he pays Mr Schneider $225.00 per week and the assisting artists $125.00 per week which even Mr Wagner will say makes $350.00 a week and that the engagement lasts from October 1 to May 18 the following year. Mr McCormack sincerely hopes Mr Wagner pays his employees as fair a wage, and would remind Mr Wagner that he [McCormack] has no recollection of having ever criticised the wage sheet of said Mr Wagner.

Mr John McCormack presents his compliments to Mr Wagner and hopes he has made himself perfectly plain and with the necessary respect for the person and wishes of Mr Wagner.

McCormack was not one who cared to be crossed. The pianist Ivor Newton remembered that he could use 'language so earthy that a docker might have blushed to hear him'. He had his moments with Wagner and tended not to be too well disposed towards other tenors as Richard Crooks discovered when, at the end of an opera performance, McCormack congratulated the cast in person – with the exception of Crooks. This was all the more unfortunate as Crooks greatly admired McCormack and was bitterly hurt.

A major grievance McCormack had with Wagner was the agent's arrangement with some concert halls whereby McCormack could only be booked if other singers on Wagner's books got concerts too. That way Wagner could diminish some of the risk of his business while promoting some of his lesser artists, though it was of no advantage to an established artist. This was probably one reason why the tenor and Wagner eventually parted, although they remained on good terms, corresponding occasionally until McCormack's death. And McCormack certainly recognised Wagner's abilities and valued the way he had been managed. An envelope he sent from the Hotel Muehlebach, Kansas City, Missouri, on 29th January 1919, was addressed to 'the one and only world-famed indefatigable town moving manager – Charles L Wagner, 511 Fifth Ave, New York'. McCormack was not one to say or do

They called themselves the three musketeers: McCormack (centre), accompanist Teddy Schneider (right) and road manager Denis F McSweeney (left). 'Mac' took over as McCormack's sole manager in the mid-1920s.

things by halves. He gave praise where praise was due: a telegram from St Louis to Wagner, dated February 1919, reads: 'You are right I think I put St Louis on the map. One of the greatest ovations of my career and I sang splendidly. My congratulations on your managerial perspicacity. Regards, John McCormack.' Ironically, given that St Louis was where McCormack had first sung in America way back in 1904, the town for some unexplained reason did not react initially with the enthusiasm found elsewhere. Wagner's persistence and promotional work had paid off.

Yet despite the enthusiasm and appreciation McCormack could show for Wagner's skills, he had more fellow feeling for Denis McSweeney, a Kerry man who had worked with the Wolfsohn Bureau before going to work for Charles L Wagner. McSweeney had heard McCormack during his Manhattan Opera days and much admired what he heard. According to Wagner: 'McSweeney's ardent devotion to John still annoyed the singer at times and was disliked by Mrs McCormack and her sister, Miss Foley…' But Marie Narelle, an Irish singer and one-time assistant artist to McCormack, perceived McSweeney's qualities and recommended him to Wagner, who took him on. He toured with McCormack and Schneider, they called themselves 'the three Musketeers' and 'Mac' became one of McCormack's closest associates. He eventually took over sole management of the tenor and the partnership ended only with McSweeney's death in 1934.

In the spring of 1914, with his management in place, and with his new accompanist, McCormack sang a further fifty concerts followed by no less than ninety-five concerts over the 1914–15 season. This was his most intense schedule, and one that Lily refused to allow him to repeat for fear of the toll on his health. But the reductions he made were minimal and the strain often showed. McCormack was not one to hide it. From the Hotel Sheldon-Munn in Ames, Iowa, on 25th October 1919, he wrote to Wagner:

Dear Charles:

May God forgive you putting me in this most superjerk-water-town for I never can. Oh the eats! Imagine if you can a dining-room that closes at 1:30 mid-day for lunch why even in the hash-houses I lived in [in] my younger days never closed at such [an] hour but I guess that they get up so early in Iowa that they want food early. We leave after the concert thank God. My wish to you is that you get the same rotten food that we get here and that you don't sleep for a week as we didn't here.

Regards, nevertheless. John McCormack.

And this was no isolated outburst. From Hutchinson, Kansas, in an undated letter, he wrote to Wagner at length, spelling out his difficulties:

Dear Charles L,

This is certainly the limit when it comes to towns and you have given me some awful ones. The trip from St Louis to Oklahoma City was hell, no dining car and breakfast at seven o'clock in the morning, and the lunch!!!! My God! Then from Tulsa to here no drawing-room and there never was one on the Wichita car. Then trying to snatch a sandwich in a section after a hard concert, then two and half hours on trolley car. Now Charles this won't suit me it may be all right for a Chautauqua troope but not for mine. Of course you may blame the R.R. administration but you must not make your journeys harder when the R.R. accommodations get worse. This is not the way things are done.

I notice that I arrive Lincoln the noon of the day of the concert. This is monstrous, not fair to me or the public and I hereby give notice if there is not a drawing-room to Lincoln, there will be *no* concert and I will go direct to Chicago… I give you my word that some more jumps and tours like this present [one] would soon stop my singing.

Can't I make you see that a tenor voice – although perhaps as some Hun said it may be a disease – is a very delicate organ and not a *machine*. I will sing every second day for eight months if you don't give me a journey of more than eight hours between… if you won't take my voice into consideration I will just have to do so myself and in our next contract (if any!) put a clause in that the towns and dates be put up to me for my O.K. Now a last word of advice don't write me a smart letter so that you can say 'that ought to hold John for a while'. Two of us can do that and I'll back myself. Just give this your sympathetic attention it is not meant as a kick it is just a protest (subtle difference) from a very tired tenor.

Regards yours, John McCormack.

So much for the glamour of touring. Even to consider singing every other day, no matter how short the trip between concerts, was preposterous. No singer would consider doing so now. The pressure on McCormack was enormous, as everyone wanted to hear him in person.

Through the concert format, McCormack became a phenomenon of his times. How else to describe the enormous appeal he exerted wherever he sang? Newsclips

HUGE AUDIENCES WELCOME McCORMACK TO SOUTH

Famous Tenor Delighted with Experiences of Recent Southern Tour—Winter Plans Include Chicago Opera Appearances and Concerts in the West

CONVINCED that Southern hospitality is a delightful reality, John McCormack, the distinguished Irish tenor, has returned from a trip which took him to New Orleans, Texas and other points, enthusiastic over the reception given to him by his audiences and everyone he met, socially and professionally. In many of the cities he visited he was formally received by members of the city government and he admits that if he had accepted all the invitations for luncheons and dinners extended to him he would not have been able to sing a note.

In every city visited on this trip the local managers made requests for not one but two dates for next season. The tour from beginning to end was a complete triumph for Mr. McCormack.

The first engagement was in Washington, D. C., Nov. 26, when he filled the New National Theater to its capacity. Throughout the tour ...ity houses were decidedly in evidence. In almost every place the entire house had been sold out days before the concert. It was n Dallas, Tex., that one McCormack enthusiast who had been disappointed in ....

daily papers for seats, indicating the location desired and that the question of price did not enter into the transaction.

Visits One of Youngest Cities

Mr. McCormack had the interesting experience of singing in Tulsa, Okla., one of the youngest cities in the country, being fifteen years old. Here the concert was given under the auspices of the Hyechka Woman's Club.

In Fort Worth, Tex., it was announced after the concert that the financial returns had been so ample that the entire series given by the Harmony Club would not result in a deficit this season, as had sometimes been the case. In Austin, Tex., Mr. McCormack found what he termed the most enthusiastic audience before which he ever appeared. Before he left there a delegation from Dallas called upon him for the purpose of trying to induce him to ar nge for another

date in Dallas this season. He sang in Houston and in New Orleans. He sang in the l**ter city the scale of prices charged for s. was on the Metropolitan Opera Co. any basis, ranging from $5 down with tanding room at $2.

In .nuary Mr. McCormack will sing in three performances with the Chicago Opera Co. in Chicago, the operas being "La Bohème" and "Don Giovanni." He will also give a concert in Chicago and will be heard later in January in Pittsburgh and Cincinnati. During February he will be in the West.

McCormack at New Orleans

NEW ORLEANS, LA., Dec. 18.—On Monday night John McCormack, the celebrated tenor, made his first appearance before the New Orleans public, and not for many seasons has there been such an enthusiastic audience to greet a singer

as that which filled the Athenæum to overflowing. Long before the date announced for the opening of the box office the house was practically sold out and at the last moment hundreds of music lovers purchased general admission tickets and stood in the aisles of the upper galleries throughout the entire program.

Delight in Irish Folk Songs

Mr. McCormack was in splendid voice, and, living up to his reputation, was quite generous in encores. The program opened with two old classics of Handel, "Where'er You Walk" and "Tell Fair Irene," followed by songs from the modern school, Bleichmann, Sjögren, MacDowell and Tschaikowsky, but it was the Irish folk songs, "As I Went a-Walking," "Lagan Love Song," "The Ballynure Ballad" and "The Cruiskeen Lawn," that carried the audience into ed applause and nothing less than ncores

would satisfy them. His last group commenced with "When the Dew Is Falling," by Edwin Schneider, Mr. McCormack's able accompanist, who rose to receive the applause justly due him; "The Old Refrain," by Fritz Kreisler (a Viennese song, arranged and dedicated to Mr. McCormack), and "If You Would Love Me," by James G. MacDermid, but the continual applause brought Mr. McCormack back for another encore. At the close thousands left the auditorium reluctantly and with the hope that the great tenor would come back again next season.

Donald McBeath's violin numbers on the program were well received, and only overshadowed by the popularity of Mr. McCormack. It is needless to add that the audience was thrilled with Edwin Schneider's perfect accompaniments. One fine day we hope to hear Mr. Schneider in solos.   D. B. F.

McCORMACK FURORE IN SAN FRANCISCO

Great Tenor Attracts Clamoring Throngs of Listeners —"Pop" Concert—Trio Heard—Auditorium Music

John McCormack achieved as great a success in San Francisco, judged by attendance and applause, as can be possible. The entire seating capacity of the great Exposition Auditorium was sold out in advance of the performance, and the day before the opening of the concert by McCormack it was impossible to buy a ticket for a seat, notwithstanding that, in addition to thousands of permanent seats, a great number of temporarily placed chairs were secured to give the people from a score of cities and towns surrounding San Francisco a chance to hear McCormack's singing. When the auditorium doors were opened this afternoon, some time in advance of the hour set for McCormack to sing, great crowds clamored for standing room only and would have paid large prices for the same rather than to have been shut out by lack of more capacity to accommodate them. A force of seventy-five ushers was employed to seat the great audience, and the doors were opened an hour before the opening hour of the concert to avoid a jam at the entrance doors.

Notwithstanding that McCormack was still troubled with a cold his voice had compelling beauty, and his wonderful enunciation and charm of style, and human sympathy, caused the enthusiasm to increase to the end. When the program, with many encores, had been completed, an audience of thousands refused to move from the seats until the singer ave them, as a parting song, "Drink to Me Only."

M CORMACK SINGS TO 4,000 AT CENTURY

Adds Comic "Kitty, Won't You Marry Me?" to His Irish Folksongs and Ballads.

Four thousand admirers of John McCormack filled the big Century Theatre to overflowing in yesterday's first Winter storm. When advance indications of a crowd appeared, the stage was hastily cleared of its mountains of Max Reinhardt's scenery. Even so, there were several hundred late-comers turned away from the matinee.

Newsclippings of the day tell the tale. The tenor was mobbed wherever he went.

RECORD RICHMOND AUDIENCE GREETS McCORMACK.

Return Engagement of Irish Tenor—Over $5,000 Gross Receipts Taken In.

Richmond, Va., February 19, 1916.

Not in the musical chronicles of this city has there been accorded to a visiting artist on a return engagement such a reception in point of numbers and enthusiasm as that given February 15 at the Auditorium, to the Irish tenor, John McCormack. For the first time since it developed from a market house into a concert hall, so far as the memory of one man can recall, the City Auditorium's vast floor and deep balcony were not large enough to accommodate the crowds that clamored to buy seats, and chairs were sold on the stage.

He opened the program with two superb Handel arias, both of which he sang in magnificent style, displaying the undoubted beauty of his voice and a breath control not short of amazing. The program contained also a group of four songs by Schubert, Schumann, Rachmaninoff and Tschaikowsky. His rendition of these completely captivated his audience, and he was forced to give several encores. The rollicking "Nelly My Love, and Me," concluded the group of Irish songs, but not according to the idea of the audience. The house took matters into its own hands and encore after encore was compelled and generously given. From the opening Handel numbers to the closing song, not only the pit, but the balcony, rose at him and when he had finished the house actually rose and remained standing, applauding and even cheering until he came back and sang again.

Edwin Schneider, the accompanist, provided such support, both to Mr. McCormack and to Mr. McBeath as soloists rarely are able to obtain.

Mr. McBeath's playing was well received.

The concert was given under the local management of W. H. Betts, who brought Mr. McCormack to Richmond last year. This was a night of triumph for Manager Betts,

of the day speak for themselves: 'McCormack's Fifth Greater New York Recital of Season – huge audience seems insatiate'; 'McCormack furore in San Francisco – great tenor attracts clamoring throngs'; 'St Paul box office records broken'; 'Record Richmond audience greets McCormack, return engagement of Irish tenor'. Such newspaper headings are typical; and it is probably true to say that, by the middle war years, with few exceptions, McCormack could fill any auditorium throughout the States to capacity and indeed over capacity. Not only standing room, but seats on the stage grouped around the singer became the norm – he would visit Chicago four times a year, singing a different programme each time; he filled San Francisco's Civic Auditorium twice over in one week. In Boston, a great Irish stronghold of course, he would appear up to four times at Symphony Hall inside a *single week*.

In New York, the atmosphere surrounding a McCormack appearance in 1916 at Carnegie Hall is vividly described by the *Musical Courier* on 20th January:

> If one were to judge from the crowds that frantically endeavoured to get into the building, filling every box and seat in the house, overflowing on to the stage, and occupying every bit of standing room which the fire laws permitted, said judge would undoubtedly have concluded that the celebrated Irish tenor was about to retire and might never sing again in public; while on the contrary, he is announced for another appearance in the same hall on February 13.

146

ST. PAUL BOX OFFICE RECORDS BROKEN BY JOHN McCORMACK.

Irish Tenor Draws Usual Vast Throng of Admirers—Percy Grainger Makes Initial Local Appearance and Scores Success.

St. Paul, Minn., February 9, 1916.

St. Paul's musical high lights of the past week were Percy Grainger and John McCormack. The former came as one of the Schubert Club artist attractions for the season, and the latter sang under the auspices (locally) of Edmund A. Stein, assistant manager of the Minneapolis Symphony Orchestra.

Great interest naturally attached to the first appearance here of the young Australian composer-pianist, and the majority sentiment is extremely flattering to him. The most beautiful and remarkable performance of the Grainger program was Ravel's "Ondine," of which the pianist made an exquisite picture. His tone and coloring were perfect, and the whimsical, plaintive imagery of the wee episode was charmingly indicated.

Two Debussy numbers were also very enjoyable, and the Grieg folksong and dance had splendid vigor and rhythm. The concert opened with the Bach-Busoni prelude and fugue in D major, the performance of which was interesting, and the pianist's own compositions included the "Colonial Song," which is a pleasant improvisation. The concert was delightful, and a return engagement here would unquestionably prove popular.

McCORMACK'S BIG AUDIENCE.

5000 HEAR M'CORMACK IN HIS THIRD RECITAL

500 Chairs on Stage and 300 in Orchestra Pit Filled

RECEIPTS TOTAL $7000

John McCormack's third recital of this season at the Metropolitan Opera House last night was attended by nearly 5000 persons—probably the largest audience ever attracted to that big auditorium in the eight years of its existence by a single artist.

Not only was every seat in the house occupied, but 500 chairs on the stage and 300 chairs in the orchestra pit were filled before the concert began. And lining the brass rails at the rear of the parquet were several hundred standees. It is estimated that the receipts for the recital approximated $7000.

Mr. McCormack's program began with "Aubade Le Roi d'Ys," an exotic number by Lalo, and the finale to the third act of Leoncavallo's "Boheme," a high-pitched number little suited either to Mc-

McCormack would move between Carnegie Hall, the Metropolitan Opera, and the mighty New York Hippodrome in the same season, creating at each the same frantic rush for seats. As *The North American* in Philadelphia reported on 29th April 1916:

> John McCormack's third recital of this season at the Metropolitan Opera House last night was attended by nearly 5,000 persons. [It was] probably the largest audience ever attracted to that big auditorium. Not only was every seat in the house occupied, but 500 chairs on the stage and 300 chairs in the orchestra pit were filled before the concert began. And lining the brass rails at the rear of the parquet were several hundred standees.

He played the New York Hippodrome eight or ten times a season. In the 1915–16 season, McCormack gave twelve concerts in New York without repeating a single item, except in the case of encores. America had never seen any thing like it.

The mighty New York Hippodrome on 28th April 1918 in which there were 5,000 seated in the auditorium, 1,000 seated on the stage and a further 1,000 standees. The tenor and Teddy Schneider can just be seen at the front of the stage.

'He has become a national institution,' declared *The Pictorial Review* in 1916 and, if proof of this was needed, it came with the Fourth of July celebrations in 1918, when, as *Musical America* reported:

> …he was invited by the committee in charge of the Fourth of July celebration in Washington to participate in the historic meeting held on the grassy Potomac slope where the Father of His Country is buried. The invitation was extended following a conference between George Creel, chairman of the committee and President Wilson.
>
> It was the one hundred and forty-second anniversary of the signing of the Declaration of Independence, and the meeting will go down as one of the most important in the history of this country because of the great speech ('a new Declaration of Independence') delivered by a great President, and because of the representative character of the gathering.

Thirty-three nationalities were represented. As each pilgrim passed by President Wilson to lay a wreath on the tomb of Washington, as a token of fealty to the principles laid down by the Father of His Country, Mr McCormack, standing by his side, sang 'The Battle Hymn of the Republic'. Later on, following the President's great speech, the singer mounted a slight eminence to one side of the tomb and sang 'The Star Spangled Banner'. Soldiers, sailors and marines to the number of 1,000 stood at salute, and the thousands of citizens who were crowded on to the lawn were thrilled by the noted tenor's spirited rendition of the national anthem.

Mr McCormack was a guest of the President on board the *Mayflower* on the trip from Washington to Mount Vernon and return, and President Wilson extended his congratulations, warmly grasping the singer by the hand and telling him it was the finest rendition of our anthem he had ever heard.

The honour was all the more exceptional in that McCormack was not, at the time, an American citizen. He had applied for citizenship in April 1914. The process required an interval of five years before his citizenship was ratified, which it was in June 1919. Among the requirements of American citizenship is the obligation, three years after the initial application, to renounce all existing loyalties. For McCormack, this required renouncing loyalty to the British crown. As an Irish nationalist, he is unlikely to have felt any personal conflict in renouncing a loyalty to an English king whose dominion over Ireland he did not approve of. On 27th January 1917, *The Times* made the simple announcement that 'the Irish tenor has renounced his allegiance to King George V and declared his intention of becoming a citizen of the United States', and made no further comment. But feelings ran high during the First World War and the spirit of the times was very much a case of: if you are not for us, then you must be against us. McCormack became the object of hate mail and obloquy. It should have been obvious that so overt an action as renunciation of loyalty to the crown would produce some reaction. He had after all done well by Covent Garden. He had participated in the Gala performance at the Royal Opera celebrating the coronation of the same king as recently as 1911. He had moved in establishment circles and had made the most of it. The likelihood is not that McCormack expected no reaction, rather that he greatly underestimated it.

To say the least, Lily McCormack was circumspect about her husband's application for American citizenship and had remarkably little to say about it. She records but one conversation on the subject that took place after his American tour of 1913:

This letter was published in The Musical Courier *and very likely elsewhere as part of the war effort in America. Its recipient was Michael Keane of the musical publishers Boosey & Co. and reads: My dear Michael, I am so glad the good public liked our war song 'God be with the Boys'. It is a real prayer and one I feel certain that finds an echo in every American heart. I sincerely hope a copy of the splendid ballad will find a place in every American home.'*

John said to me, 'I wonder if you feel as I do, Lily, that our home is *really* here in the United States.'

I said, 'Darling, you know that wherever *you* are is home to me.'

'I know that my future is here,' he went on, 'and if you are sure it's all right with you, I'd like to become an American citizen.' I was not surprised.

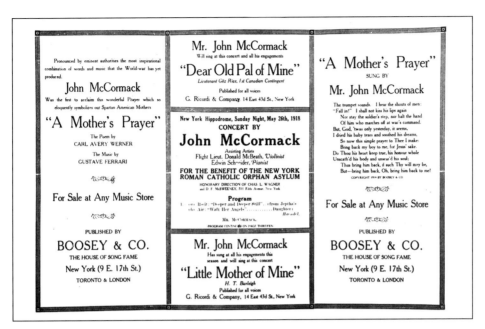

Concert for the benefit of the New York Roman Catholic Orphan Asylum, New York Hippodrome, 26th May 1918. The tenor opened with the recitative and aria from Jeptha's Daughter *by Handel; but what the audience most wanted to hear may be judged from the advertisements surrounding the programme.*

Of any political motivation behind the application or the tax benefits of being an American citizen, *I Hear You Calling Me* contains nothing. The tenor's agent in London, Thomas Quinlan, went on record saying that the decision was made purely for financial reasons. At any rate, in England, McCormack became *persona non grata* and, for ten years, he did not sing in London or anywhere in England. And these were some of the best years of his career.

However, when America entered the war in 1917, McCormack offered his services to President Wilson who reckoned that, as a singer, he would be better remaining in America – 'keeping the fountains of sentiment flowing' – rather than joining a troop ship. He then entered the war effort with zest, raising prodigious sums of money for charities; undertaking a coast-to-coast concert tour of the States on behalf of the Red Cross at his own expense. He sang songs chosen by members of the audience, for which they were required to pay high prices; his autographed records were auctioned for charity. It is said that he raised $500,000 for the Liberty Bond Drive.

There is no question that he put his back into the war effort at considerable expense and effort to himself, always looking for novel ways to help charities. A flurry of telegrams show how seriously he took his charitable work. In one, he writes to Amelita Galli-Curci in his own idiosyncratic Italian, to which the Postal Telegraph Company then added their own confusing touches.

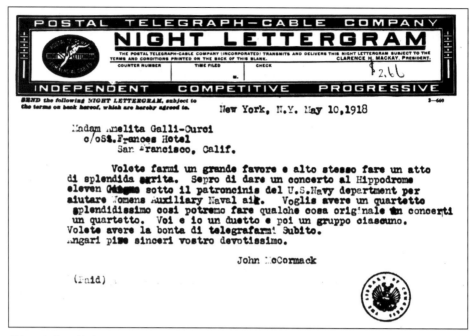

Telegram from McCormack to Amelita Galli-Curci dated 10th May 1918. The Italian got rather tangled in the despatch.

To: Madam Amelita Galli-Curci, c/o St Frances Hotel, San Francisco, California from NY May 10, 1918.

Volete farmi un grande favore e alto stesso fare un atto di splendida carita. Sepro di dare un concerto al Hippodrome eleven Giugno sotto il patroncinis del U.S. Navy department per aiutare Womens Auxiliary Naval aid. Voglis avere un quartetto splendissimo cosi potremo fare qualche cosa originale un concerti un quartetto. Voi e io un duetto e poi un gruppo ciascuno. Volete avere la bonta di telegrafarmi Subito. Angari piu sinceri vostro devotissimo, John McCormack.

[Would you please do me a great favour and at the same time a splendid act of charity. I hope to give a concert at the Hippodrome on June 11th under the patronage of the US Navy Department's Women's Auxiliary Aid. I want to have a splendid quartet… you and I can give a duet and then a group each. Please send me a telegram immediately. Sincere greetings, yours devotedly, John McCormack.]

Galli-Curci replied in the negative, and McCormack's next telegram to her, dated 14th May, and written in English, leaves no doubt as to his feelings:

> Madam Amelita Galli-Curci, c/o Alexandria Hotel, Los Angeles, California
>
> Sorry you are so tired. So am I. So are the soldiers and sailors for whom the concert was meant. I have forwarded your telegram to Washington. John McCormack.

And he followed this up with a bitter telegram to Charles L Wagner on 16th May:

> It's bad enough to have Galli-Curci refuse to appear at a great United States charity. But don't for goodness sake tell deliberate lies to shield her... Am more hurt than I can say at this flagrant ingratitude as you know I am tired but what is our little tiredness compared to those who are fighting for us in the trenches and on the high seas.
>
> Regards,
> John McCormack.

His records were favourites with the American soldiers. He recorded a number of songs associated with the war, including 'Keep the Home Fires Burning' (1917) and 'God be with our Boys in Picardy Tonight' (1918). A notable favourite with the troops

McCormack singing at an open-air concert during the First World War. The pose was characteristic.

153

A study in moods. The tenor with his lifelong friend Archbishop Curley who also came from Athlone. Curley played a large part in shaping McCormack's first biography, consisting of narrative passages with linking interviews written up by Pierre Key.

was 'Mother Machree' which McCormack had recorded in 1911. It is a song that has nothing directly to do with war; but the subject of motherhood often becomes a pre-occupation with men facing severe hardship or death and the song struck a particular chord with the armed forces.

In 1918, the first biography of McCormack appeared: *John McCormack: His Own Life Story*, prompted by Charles L Wagner who saw the publicity value of such an enterprise. It is largely drawn on interviews with the tenor and 'transcribed' by the journalist Pierre V R Key during visits to Rocklea, McCormack's house in Connecticut. Transcriptions or not, McCormack was dissatisfied with the end result and bought out as much of the first edition as he could. There was a third party to the book – McCormack's friend of old, Bishop Michael Curley, who became an adviser to the project. As a result, in Wagner's words, the: '…entire idea was altered. What was intended to be an authentic story turned out a very sentimental and unreal account.' It was also an idealised account with any sharp edges carefully smoothed off.

McCormack's attitude to Curley, a man of 'the cloth', was meek and deferential in a way that was not typical of the tenor in other circumstances. This comes across in McCormack's correspondence with Curley, which the tenor liked to pepper with references to 'Your Grace'.

> During my stay in Germany I tried every means in my power to try and get the management of the Hotel and even the proprietor himself to serve a glass of French wine but without avail. I did this of course as Your Grace will understand – not because I particularly like a glass of champagne – but to see whether the feeling against all things French…

Nevertheless, the book is of interest being the first account of the tenor's life. One other biography was published during the tenor's lifetime – just at the end of his life – L A G Strong's *John McCormack*. McCormack wrote to Charles L Wagner from Woodend, South Ascot, England on 11th September 1940, asking Wagner for two copies of his own autobiography *Seeing Stars* and then goes on to say: 'By a curious coincidence I just finished my memoirs in collaboration with L A G Strong the novelist and Methuen is bringing it out here. I think it is good and *very kind*.' It provides an overview of McCormack's life and contains what few other biographies on singers do, namely some of McCormack's views on the singing of singers he had known.

Lily experienced a personal tragedy in the closing stages of the war when her brother Thomas and his wife Charlotte went down on the mailboat *Leinster*, which was torpedoed in Dublin Bay en route to Holyhead in Wales in October 1918. They were travelling for the worst possible reason. Word had come through that Charlotte's brother had been seriously wounded (fatally in fact) and they were travelling to England intending to see him.

When the news came through of Thomas' and Charlotte's death, Lily recorded that: 'We all sat there in numb silence. Aunty and I could only think of their children, five boys and five girls, all under sixteen.' Lily's mother had taken the children in and John immediately arranged for them to get a larger house. He supported the children until they reached adulthood and the McCormacks legally adopted the youngest, Kevin, then only sixteen months old and, as Lily recalled: 'Somewhat to our surprise, but also to our joy, we started all over again with a nursery, a pram and "Nanny".'

McCormack, despite his phenomenal international success, had not forgotten Athlone or indeed Ireland in general. He sang charity concerts for the Irish White Cross Fund. Proceeds from a massive concert at the New York Hippodrome on 13th May 1917 for 'The French Tuberculosis Soldiers' Relief Fund and Athlone Ireland

"A Studied Insult"

Famous Tenor Arrives

"ATTEMPT TO EMBARRASS ME"

As Mr John M'Cormack, the famous tenor, stepped on to the Spencer street station from the Adelaide express this morning and joyfully acknowledged the salutations of a number of friends he did not look as if he had been the victim of "a studied insult" in the capital of South Australia. His face was wreathed in smiles and he grasped the hands of his friends affectionately.

"How are you, John?" asked Mr J. Tait, as he held out his hand, and the reply was that he was all right. The tenor was touched by the greetings, and temperament showed itself again when the abrupt closing of the Adelaide season was mentioned. Mr M'Cormack's face became overcast, and he emphatically declared that a studied insult was offered to him on Thursday evening by a small section of the audience at the Exhibition Building, Adelaide, and that he had suffered indignities elsewhere.

"The Obvious Insinuation"

"You do not know all," remarked Mr M'Cormack as the question was asked whether the singing of the National Anthem by a few people should have been sufficient to induce him to abandon his final concert in Adelaide.

"It was a studied insult," said Mr M'Cormack, "because of the obvious insinuation that I had refused either to sing the National Anthem or have it performed. Such an insinuation of a breach of common courtesy I consider a grave insult. I would not refuse to sing the anthem of any country in

A Sensitive Tenor

Cancellation of Tour

Until as late as yesterday afternoon the Melbourne admirers of Mr John M'Cormack believed that the famous tenor, in spite of the ill-feeling engendered by the singing of the National Anthem in Adelaide, would fulfil the remainder of his engagements in Australia, and would sing, as advertised, in the Melbourne Town Hall on Saturday night.

A "Herald" representative was definitely told by Mr M'Sweeney, the tenor's manager, yesterday, that there was no intention of cancelling the concert in the Melbourne Town Hall on Saturday night. It was explained today, however, that at the time of this assurance it had not been definitely decided that Mr M'Cormack's tour would not be continued.

Apparently the singer's Town Hall engagement was finally cancelled on Tuesday night. Mr Hubert Leslie's company, which had originally booked the Town Hall for Saturday night and the following Tuesday, Thursday, and Saturday, but had made way for Mr John M'Cormack, were notified on Tuesday night that they were now able, as originally promised, to use the hall as from Saturday night, the tenor's engagement having lapsed.

Mr M'Cormack and Mr M'Sweeney left by last evening's express for Sydney.

Australian newsclippings

Relief Fund', were sent by the tenor to Athlone for poor relief, many having suffered from the previous harsh winter. He made but one stipulation: that the committee set up for the dispersal of funds should consist of both Protestants and Roman Catholics: 'A magnificent gesture worthy of the best Christian motives.' Such a committee was indeed set up but matters became tangled thereafter. An impression circulated that funds had been misappropriated, used by small businessmen in the town to pay off debts, so that the truly needy did not receive what was intended for them. The poor got free potatoes. But in his book *John McCormack and Athlone* local historian Gearoid O'Brien suggests that:

On examination of the facts this would seem to be little more than mere fabrication… there is no evidence to suggest that they [the funds] were not used to the best advantage. It may well have happened that some businessman was bailed but if so it was probably a genuinely needy case. There may have been an element of parochial jealousy in the rumours that circulated.

But the damage was done. Although he came out of retirement to sing on behalf of the Red Cross during the Second World War, McCormack did not respond to a request to sing a concert in Athlone on behalf of those who had lost their livelihood on account of a disastrous fire at the Woollen Mills in 1940. Nor did he include Athlone in the farewell tour in 1938 that took him around Ireland.

Long before that, he had to deal with repercussions following his taking of American citizenship. Feelings extended beyond England and went on after the war. A concert tour of Australia in 1920 started well enough but there were undertones of what was to follow. McCormack wrote to Wagner in good spirits from The Oriental Hotel in Melbourne on 5th September.

Let me explain that the only reason you are getting a letter is because there is nothing else to do on a Sunday… Just imagine no train leaves Sydney for Melbourne on Saturday night because it would break the Sabbath by arriving in the state of Victoria on Sunday. Believe me the Pilgrim Fathers were pikers. Well business here is phenomenal I have done ten concerts in Sydney and eight in Melbourne and I do four in Adelaide and then return for five more in both Melbourne and Sydney. The audiences are fine, most enthusiastic and very cultured and most interested in any new music that is brought before them. Of course that section of the community who hate everything American are still very bitter but they are a very small and nasty minority and they have done everything to make my life a hell here. Please keep this entirely to yourself as I intend when I get back to God's own country to have a few things to say.

Things came to a head in Adelaide, less than a week after McCormack had written to Wagner, *The Times* reported that:

Owing to the omission of the National Anthem at Mr John McCormack's, the Irish tenor's, concerts, a large crowd made a demonstration. Hundreds remained behind at the conclusion. Someone shouted 'Sinn Féin'. 'God Save the King' was sung while the tenor was preparing to depart.

Mr McCormack was visibly affected by the imputation of disloyalty, and has refused to appear in further concerts at Adelaide. It may involve the abandonment of the rest of his Australian tour. He is reported to be hurrying back to America.

The Irish faction and McCormack supporters on the one hand and those described as supporters of 'empire' on the other were spoiling for a fight. It proved impossible for the tenor to continue and the tour was cancelled. The long letter McCormack wrote to Wagner from Sydney on 2nd October 1920 paints a picture of deep bitterness:

> My Dear Charlie,
> Doubtless Mac [Denis McSweeney] has told you all the news of my final cancellation of the whole damn tour here so there is no further need for me to labour the question. I have only the most peculiar feelings in regard to this place. I have never seen such splendid loyalty and friendship on the one side and on the other the most outrageous rudeness and boorishness and discourtesy. Of course the people from whom I have received the latter treatment are now very anxious to make it appear that they did not mean to insult me for being an American but only for renouncing my allegiance to the empire. This is cutting things rather fine. There is no doubt that they have never forgiven me for becoming an American and in fact one man said in public that they would forgiven me if I had become anything but a 'damn Yank'.

He continued:

> We sail… on Wednesday D.V. and should arrive in London about the 20th November and will be at the Carlton. I think however all mail would be safer at the American Express as we may take a place as soon as we arrive there. [Thomas] Quinlan [McCormack's London agent] writes most enthusiastically about things in England and I feel sure all will be well there. By the way I see it reported that the Met intend to have a season of Opera at Covent Garden next summer. Tell Gatti I would very much like to sing there with the Company and that the fee I will

leave to himself. Of course the Covent Garden crowd do not want
me there now but I would love to put one across them by appearing with the Metropolitan Co. Some stunt boy put it over!

Quinlan's optimism was misplaced and McCormack never sang at Covent Garden
again. His eagerness, even desperation, to sing there is revealed not only by his hope
of getting in the back door, so to speak, with the Met, but by letting the Met's manager, Giulio Gatti-Casazza, set the fee. This was not at all typical of McCormack
who, by this time, was very much concerned with his earnings as his many of his
exchanges, some quite heated, with Wagner indicate.

Having put Australia behind him – and he never returned – McCormack looked
to engagements where the issue of nationality would not be raised. His letter
to Wagner from Sydney then goes on to reveal that he and Lily had a superstitious
side:

> Lily was told by a fortune teller the other day that I am to make
> a great success in Stockholm and such places in the North so I
> will expect to hear that you have fixed some dates there.
> Certainly there will have to be some success at least socially there
> to make up for the terrible time we have had here where we have
> been socially ostracised and avoided as one avoids lepers. I am
> glad however to have suffered that for being an Irishman and an
> American. It is cheap at the price.

Having decided that the risk of singing in London was too great, he took himself
off to Paris to sing, and met up with James Joyce for the first time since 1904. In
the interval Joyce, the singer *manqué*, had closely followed his countryman's
spectacular career.

On hearing McCormack in Paris in 1920, Joyce wrote him a warm letter of congratulations on his recital:

> In the general confusion the other afternoon I had not an
> opportunity to tell you how delighted we were by your singing,
> especially the aria from *Don Giovanni* ['Il mio tesoro']. I have
> lived in Italy practically ever since we last met but no Italian lyrical
> tenor that I know (Bonci possibly excepted) could do such a feat
> of breathing and phrasing – to say nothing of the beauty of tone
> in which I am glad to see, Roscommon [County Westmeath in
> fact] can leave the peninsula a fair distance behind.

Interestingly, the distinguished singing teacher, Blanche Marchesi (1863–1940) made much the same comparison, giving it as her opinion in *A Singer's Pilgrimage* that: 'As concerns refined style and art Jean de Reske, McCormack and Bonci were Caruso's superiors.'

McCormack's opera days were not quite over. Covent Garden would not employ him, but he had an invitation from Raoul Gunsbourg to appear at the Opéra de Monte Carlo in the spring of 1921. Surprisingly, he was at first reluctant to accept. He wrote to Wagner from Claridges Hotel in Paris on 8th December 1920:

> …along comes Gunsbourg and insists that I sing the season in Monte Carlo. You won't believe it but I refused for a long time and he was so pressing in his invitation and made such a good offer for Monte Carlo that on the advice of my better half I gave in and I have engaged myself to do ten performances… I cabled you the other day to come over for the season at Monte Carlo and spend some of that fortune of yours and take a rest. God knows you need it and down there you won't be able to worry about towns and managers and of course singers and their vagaries (whatever the hell they are).

Following successful charity concerts in Paris, McCormack sang six concerts in Monte Carlo and appeared in the first ever production there of *Die Zauberflöte* on 26th March 1921, in a cast that included Graziella Pareto, followed by performances in *Tosca* with Gilda Dalla Rizza and Dingh Gilly, and *Il Barbiere di Siviglia* with Pareto as Rosina, Ernesto Badini as Figaro and Vanni Marcoux as Bartolo. The Monte Carlo Opera House only seats about 500, ideal for a singer whose virtues lie in refined singing. As Tamino, McCormack was described as 'an impeccable artist with an excellent method and lovely style, this tenor like whom there are few, was naturally called upon to sing Mozart'. His first appearance was a month earlier, on 26th February, as Cavaradossi in *Tosca*, quite different from Mozart, but it gave rise to one of the warmest and most perceptive critiques of his career. It was written by André Corneau in the *Journal de Monaco* on 1st March 1921:

> M. MacCormack [sic], an artist who enjoys an extraordinary celebrity in America, assumed for this first appearance the role of Mario Cavaradossi. This début was eagerly awaited. We must say at once that those who have been privileged to hear this impeccable singer at the concerts were not disappointed. The voice of M. MacCormack is not large, it is the voice of a light

McCormack and the Polish tenor Jean de Reske (1850–1925). When singing at Monte Carlo, John and Lily were entertained by the de Reskes at their villa in Nice.

tenor, extraordinarily well placed, to which study has given an incredible suppleness, a voice which the artist uses to perfection. M. MacCormack singing without trying for effect and without permitting himself the slightest blemish of bad taste, he does not just produce volume for volume's sake. He neither rushes nor retards the tempi according to caprice, and he does not hang on to high notes for interminable periods in order to win applause.

Never does he transgress the most elementary law of song, that is, absolute respect for the music as it is written, nor does he modify the contour or the significance of a piece – and what a marvellous feeling for nuance and what clear articulation. In a word, the singer with his good method and always distinguished and classic style is simply admirable. Also, the manner in which he sang the last act of *Tosca* was a real feast of delicacy.

At this time, Jean de Reske (1850–1925), the legendary Polish tenor remembered for his own refinement of style, was living in retirement in Nice and the McCormacks were entertained by de Reske and his wife at their villa. Unknown to McCormack, de Reske slipped into a performance of *Il Barbiere* and expressed his admiration for the Irishman's singing by writing to him with the now well-known phrase: 'You are the true redeemer of bel canto.' From no other singer could the praise have meant more. McCormack took time out to sing for de Reske's pupils.

McCormack's final opera appearances were also in Monte Carlo in the spring of 1923 when he again sang in *Il Barbiere di Siviglia* with Mercedes Capsir as Rosina, and in *Tosca* again with Dalla Rizza. He also sang Pinkerton in *Madama Butterfly* with Dalla Rizza in the title role and appeared with Mercedes Capsir in a single performance of Flotow's *Martha*. But his best role of the season, according to André Corneau, was that of Gritzko in N N Tcherepnin's arrangement of Mussorgsky's *La Foire de Sorotchintzi* which received its world premiere in Monte Carlo, on 17th March. 'A helluva day for an Irishman to create the art of a Russian peasant,' McCormack enthused in a letter to his manager. Indeed it was, with a strong Russian presence in Monte Carlo. But Gunsbourg's judgement was good. Corneau wrote in the *Journal de Monaco* on 20th March: 'The romance in Act 1 "Pourquoi mon triste coeur", he sang divinely with a sigh of exquisite melancholy, tinged with tenderness, quivering with nostalgic Slavonic charm.' The opera was received with tremendous enthusiasm; and it was in the role of Gritzko that McCormack sang for the very last time in opera, on 25th March 1923. 'Few singers,' wrote Tom Walsh in *Monte Carlo Opera*, 'have been acclaimed more perceptively or more fervently on their farewell appearance.'

It was an appearance that might not have taken place at all. McCormack had returned to the States for a concert tour in 1921–22 and was about to give a concert in April at the New York Hippodrome when he was struck down by a streptococcal throat infection. Lily recalled:

By midnight John was running a high temperature and by morning a severe streptococcal infection had developed. In spite of the most expert medical care he grew steadily worse. During those anxious days we had thousands of letters from people all over the country, and special prayers for his recovery were said in churches of all denominations.

By Holy Thursday, 13th April 1922, he was sinking into unconsciousness and it looked as if the worse had to be anticipated. Lily sent the children away: Cyril with young friends, Kevin was taken to the local park and Gwen was taken to the opera by their friend, the soprano Frances Alda. On the way back, Alda, but not Gwen, caught sight of an evening paper announcing – mistakenly – the tenor's death. Not until they reached the McCormacks' apartment and spoke to the doorman did Alda learn the truth.

The following day, Archbishop Hayes and his secretary were announced unexpectedly and, in Lily's words:

> Although John was almost unconscious he seemed to understand that the Archbishop was there. His Grace gave him his blessing and placed a relic in his hand saying, 'John, this is my own relic of the True Cross and I am leaving it with you until you are quite recovered. You are not to worry for you are going to get better.' John must have understood, as he wouldn't let the little relic out of his hand. That night he improved and in two days he was out of danger.

When he was back on his feet and well enough to go out, McCormack called on the archbishop to return the relic. The archbishop insisted that the tenor keep it. 'That day,' Lily wrote, 'John decided to start the Nine First Fridays over again [the resolution of attending Mass on the first Friday of every month, for nine months] – a devotion which we succeeded in completing together a total of five times during his busy years.'

John and Lily spent the summer of 1922 quietly in England, renting Netherswell Manor, Gloucestershire from Sir John Murray Scott's sisters Alicia and Mary. It would appear his American citizenship did not affect his friendship with them, the most English and establishment of friends. He was now at something of a crossroads in his career. He had reason to be worried about the state of his voice and his future. He was still resting from his illness and it would be many months before he sang again in public. This was a time for reflection and a letter he wrote to Charles L Wagner from Nether Swell Manor on 24th June 1922 gives an indication of his state of mind at this time.

My dear Charles L:

Yours from Berlin mine here. Please do believe me at least once. *I am not going back this year to work in America whether you have a hunch or not.* Let me show you a few reasons. If I go back for say twenty concerts I will have the enormous expense of the ocean travel coming to something like $7500. I will get in money from you something like $60,000 that added to my Victor check will bring my Income Tax up by $25000, so that in the last analysis I will be getting $37500 for 20 concerts. In the best analysis I will be getting $37500.00 for thirty concerts and out of pay the enormous hotel expenses and keep my apartment in New York. Charlie, I won't do it. Secondly I have had a very severe illness and I feel I need to rest until such time as I can safely do a tour without the danger of a nervous breakdown as well as a physical one.

I have worked very hard in America for many seasons and have had very little recreation. I feel that while I am young I should have the fun out of life and not wait until I am an old man. Caruso worked himself to death and what did he get out of life? As to the fickleness of the American public I disagree entirely from you. I believe that the American public likes and admires and pays to hear the artist that delivers the goods and is only fickle, if you like that word, when the artist does not deliver the goods. [This may be in response to a suggestion of Wagner's that if McCormack did not appear he would be forgotten. Wagner was to be proved right about the fickleness of the American public many years later, but for reasons other than infrequent appearances.] Believe me, if I went to America and on account of a slight cold had to cancel some concerts or sang badly for any reason or had another experience like Minneapolis then I believe the American public would become fickle and believe my voice was seriously injured by my very serious illness. There is more to life than money, besides I want a worldwide reputation.

What McCormack then goes on to say is of particular interest because it reveals that he was sensitive to the charge of being 'just a ballad singer' rather than a 'real singer', typically he puts the charge in the strongest terms:

I have made arrangements to *study* German *lieder* with Sir George Henschel this fall and Teddy and I are then going in the spring to sing in Berlin and other large German cities and Vienna and I am going to find out once for all whether I am just a Ballad singer or a *real* singer. If you were an artist you would know that to sing always for the same public is very tiresome for the singer

Another letter from Nether Swell Manor showing the tenor's state of mind after his streptococcal throat infection that nearly proved fatal.

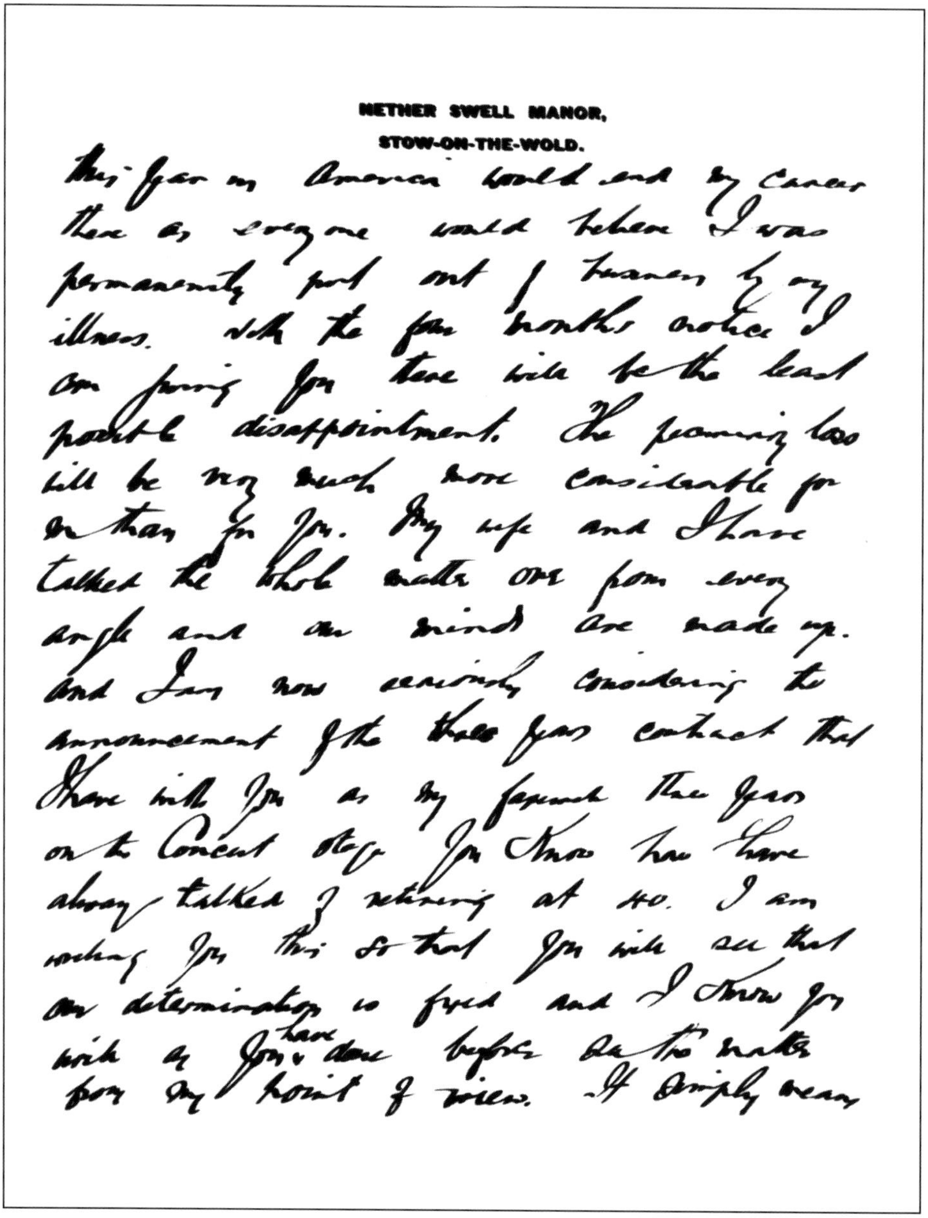

NETHER SWELL MANOR,
STOW-ON-THE-WOLD.

this year in America would end my career there as everyone would believe I was permanently put out of business by my illness. With the four months notice I am giving you there will be the least possible disappointment. The financial loss will be very much more considerable for me than for you. My wife and I have talked the whole matter over from every angle and our minds are made up. And I am now seriously considering the announcement of the three years contract that I have with you as my farewell three years on the Concert stage. You know how I have always talked of retiring at 40. I am writing you this so that you will see that our determination is fixed and I know you will as you have done before see the matter from my point of view. It simply means

and makes him inclined to be lackadaisical and slipshod in method. I want to jack myself up as it were, so that I can if possible give more to my American public that I dearly love, and I want my American public to be proud of their American singer, and to share in any successes that may be mine over here. I refuse to believe that with the American public it is a case of 'out of sight, out of mind', I protest against the libel on the most generous public in the world. I have spoken to many Americans of my decision to take the year off and they have all without a single exception, said, 'God knows you need a rest after your hard work and that heavy illness in the spring.' Therefore, Charlie, if you are writing to me again *don't try to make me change my mind for I won't do it.*

But he did change his mind; and on 15th October 1922, he returned to the New York Hippodrome. He was more than usually nervous. Lily recorded that:

> He had his usual routine concert day: light breakfast (he would *not* have it in bed) and a long walk; luncheon about 2:00; rest until 5:30; a few scales to try out his voice; dress and glance over the programme with Teddy; and a black coffee before leaving home. I always saw him to his stage dressing room to wish him good luck but never remained backstage. I can picture him now, as I closed the door, standing quietly with his rosary in his hands – always his custom before a concert.

To a packed house with standees and seats grouped round him on stage, McCormack proved his voice was intact and had one of the greatest triumphs of his career.

If McCormack was sensitive to the charge that as a singer of ballads he was not a 'real singer' as he put it, there were certainly critics who thought just that. O L Whalen in the *Detroit Journal,* for example, argued that:

> John McCormack, being from Athlone in the very heart of Ireland, and knowing the entrancing folk art of his land, could stand with Yeats and Lady Gregory as an exponent of it, and the encouragement which his audiences give should make it wonderfully agreeable, yet he chooses to sing dozens of foolish ditties and places himself only a little higher than Mary Pickford and Harold Bell Wright, who exploit the art of no country but merely purvey cheap sentimentality.

There was no question that his overwhelming success with popular ballads – never mind that he sang them with the same vocal finish and compelling musicality with which he sang everything – detracted from his reputation both during his lifetime and subsequently. The legend remains of McCormack as a singer who prostituted his greater accomplishments for commercial and sentimental material.

The fifth edition of Grove's *Dictionary of Music & Musicians* published in 1954 echoed O L Whalen's views and went even further by providing a date as to the tenor's decline in repertoire. By 1924, the dictionary, asserted:

> He could no longer be taken altogether seriously as a musician, since in his later years he devoted his extraordinary and unimpaired gifts to largely sentimental and popular ditties, not to be

listened to with patience by critics or with enjoyment by true
music lovers.

But the assertion that McCormack's concert repertoire deteriorated with the years
simply does not stand up to examination. It is true that he began as a ballad singer
around 1904, to take the date of his first recordings sessions that were devoted to ballads (although at the Feis Ceoil the previous year, he had sung Handel). But, on his
return from Italy, he could never again be described as 'nothing other than a singer
of ballads'. When he appeared with Mario Sammarco in concert at the Queen's Hall
in London on 18th October 1910, the first half of the programme was given up to
opera, with McCormack singing 'Che gelida manina' from *La Bohème* and
Sammarco 'Largo al Factotum' from *Il Barbiere di Siviglia*. Only in the second half
did McCormack introduce Irish ballads and the concert was then wound up with
the Quartet from Verdi's *Rigoletto*. During his first years in America, McCormack
followed a similar pattern. Then around 1913, with, Wagner says, his encouragement,
McCormack began to include less 19th-century opera and turned increasingly to
17th and 18th-century arias, Handel in particular, sometimes Bach; and *lieder* also
entered his repertoire. In December 1924, he outlined to *Musical America* how he
planned his concert programmes:

> The first group of songs which I give, on any programme, are
> songs which I sing to please myself. They represent my musical
> taste. The second group is made up of art songs, that is to say, fine
> songs which the public should like and which it will like once they
> are heard a sufficient number of times to become familiar.
>
> The third group I give contains the beautiful Irish folksongs
> which have survived the ages because of the deathless appeal they
> make to the hearts of men. The fourth group of songs represents
> the fine work of modern American and English composers...

The format of recitals underwent change but the diversity of material remained. He
never devoted himself exclusively to ballads, Irish or otherwise. At the Albert Hall
on 1st December 1934: 'His programme contained something of almost everything,
though modern opera was unrepresented in the scheme.' His opera days were long
behind him at this stage, instead the scheme consisted of 'setting Brahms by the sev-
enteenth century Dr Howard and Handel between Parry and Schumann...' Two
years later: 'Handel's name occurred most frequently, and it suits McCormack well,
but he also put in an example of Wolf, of Parry ('Armida's Garden') and of Franck
('Panis Angelicus').'

169

Even at the very end of his singing days, when there was not much of the voice left, appearing in Watford, England, in 1941, he sang both Handel and Rachmaninov. So however Grove and company might disapprove of some of the material he included at concerts, the fact remains that his concert repertoire always included material which, by their own standards, he might be judged a musician or not.

In fact the date of 1924, chosen by Grove, marked not the shrinking or deterioration of his repertoire but rather the expansion of it. That year, the writer and founder of *Gramophone Magazine*, Compton Mackenzie, met McCormack for the first time when the tenor was in Dublin as 'the guest of the Irish nation' during the Tailteann Games. Mackenzie recorded the meeting:

> One of the keenest pleasures in an artist's life is to be able to tell another artist quite sincerely that he admires his work. 'Yes, but I expect you think I sing a great deal of rubbish,' said McCormack to me. I agreed and suggested that for this side of the Atlantic he had sung enough. 'Yes, but I'm going to sing Wolf and Brahms now, and all sorts of songs that I really want to sing.' 'That's the best news I've heard in a long time,' I assured him.

At this point in his career, McCormack had begun developing a repertoire of German *lieder* that included songs by Wolf, Brahms and Schubert. If he did not achieve anything like the same fluency in German as he had in Italian, having come to the language so much later, his idiomatic security was remarkable. As he toured with Teddy Schneider (who was of German origin), so McCormack worked on the language. His letters sometimes contain German quotations and phrases, as if he is practising along the way. In singing, the umlaut, in particular, gave him trouble and his knowledge of German could be erratic.

He did take time out to study with Sir George Henschel (1850–1934) who was the first conductor of the Boston Symphony Orchestra, as well as being a composer, pianist, singer and author. He taught at the Royal College of Music in London. A man of deep culture, he was an excellent choice for the tenor to consult. And McCormack's reading into the German repertoire was far wider and deeper than is generally recognised. Deems Taylor retained a golden memory of an evening when 'John sang straight through two volumes of Hugo Wolf's songs, with Rachmaninoff at the piano and Ernest Newman turning the pages'.

In 1923, while England remained out of bounds, McCormack made middle Europe the focus of his career outside the States. Although it was a short tour, it took in the major cities of Prague, Paris and Berlin. Its artistic importance to McCormack

Ve čtvrtek 26. dubna 1923   SMETANOVA SÍŇ   začátek v půl 8. hod. več.

I. KONCERT
JOHN Mc. CORMACK
lyrický tenór metropolitní opery v Novém Yorku

Klavír: EDVÍN SCHNEIDER.

P O R A D:

I.
a) *Péri*: Gioite al canto mio. – Radujte se z mého zpěvu.
b) *Lotti*: Pur dicesti. – A přec jsi řekl.
c) *Händel*: O sleep, why dost thou leave me? (Semele) – O sne, proč mne opouštíš?
d) *Händel*: Enjoy the sweet Elysian Groves. (Celeste) – Raduj se v sladkých elysejských lesích.

II.
a) *Fauré*: Automne. – Podzim.
b) *Duparc*: Extase.
c) *Paladilhe*: Psyché.
d) *Chausson*: La Caravanne.

PŘESTÁVKA.

III.
a) *Rachmaninov*: How fair this spot! – Jak krásné to místo.
b) To the children – Dětem.
c) Oh cease the singing – O ustaň zpívat.
d) Fear not my love. – Neboj se mé lásky.

IV.
a) *Julius Harrison*: The las sight of Fiametta. – Poslední pohled Fiametty.
b) *Frank Bridge*: Go not happy day. – Nedávej dobrý den.
c) *Arnold Bax*: The white Peace. – Bílý mír.
d) Irská národní lidová píseň: Una Baun, upravil Hughes.

Koncertní křídlo fy. E. Steinway & Sons New York ze skladu fy. S. Kohn, Praha, Vodičkova ul.

Druhý (poslední) koncert Mc. CORMACKA koná se v pondělí 30. dubna v půl 8 h. v sále Lucerny. Na pořadu písně německé (Bach, Beethoven, Schubert, Mozart, Wolff) a irské národní písně.

Lístky v předprodeji 8–35 Kč

Berlin and Prague concert programmes from the tenor's tour of Middle Europe in 1923. He regarded this tour as one of the most important of his career as he expected to find the most discerning and critical of audiences. He triumphed.

Berlin concert 1923. Note the range of material.

Preis: 500,– Mark

KONZERT-DIREKTION HERMANN WOLFF ⬩ JULES SACHS, BERLIN W9, LINKSTR. 42

PHILHARMONIE

Mittwoch den 2. Mai 1923 – abends 8 Uhr

Lieder-Abend

John McCormack

Am Flügel: **Edwin Schneider**

I.	a) Gioite al canto mio	*Peri*
	b) Pur dicesti	*Lotti*
	c) O sleep, why dost thou leave me? (Semele)	*Händel*
	d) Enjoy the sweet Elysian Groves (Alceste)	

1st time

II.	a) Du bist die Ruh	
	b) Der Jüngling an der Quelle	
	c) Die Liebe hat gelogen	*Schubert*
	d) Dass sie hier gewesen	
	e) Entzückung an Laura	

1st time

III.	a) Verborgenheit	
	b) Im Maien	
	c) Schlafendes Jesuskind	*Hugo Wolf*
	d) Wo find' ich Trost	

— PAUSE —

Irische Volkslieder.

IV.	a) Norah O'Neale	*Arr. by Herbert Hughes*
	b) The Ballynure Ballad	
	c) My Lagan Love	*Arr. by Hamilton Harty*
	d) Una Waun	*Arr. by Karl Hardebeck*

V.	a) How fair this spot	*Rachmaninoff*
	b) To the Children	
	c) The white Peace	*Arnold Bax*
	d) A Christmas Carol	

Konzertflügel: STEINWAY ⬩ SONS, Budapester Strasse 6

Während der Vorträge bleiben die Saaltüren geschlossen

Newsclipping from The Times

McCormack

" The audience refused to leave when the lights were extinguished after a recital by John McCormack, forcing him to sing two encores in semi-darkness." So runs a wireless despatch reporting the Irish tenor's appearance in Berlin. This sort of thing certainly gives the lie to the opinion still in vogue among cynical subway riders that McCormack's reputation results from crowding audiences of servant girls and from other manifestations of Gaelic loyalty. The tenor, far from being a showy player to gushy sentiment, is one of the most refined and scholarly of artists.

He has done much to foster the present vogue of songs and other small pieces of the Italian masters of the 17th and 18th centuries, composers whose work, with its formalistic sedateness and untrumpeting beauty, is the very caviar of caviar for these jazz-blaring years.

is indicated by a letter to Charles L Wagner he wrote on 3rd March 1923 from Monte Carlo: 'As I wired you I would not think of singing the Berlin recitals between the Paris dates. I consider these recitals in Berlin as the most important things in my career and I am determined to sing as well as possible...'

The tour was as noteworthy for the critical acclaim he received as for the feverish excitement of the large crowds that he attracted, this despite there being nothing like the same number of Irish émigrés on the European continent as in the States, although he did have the benefit of a strong American contingent. John wrote to Lily from Prague on 27th April:

My Darling... I don't think I ever sang better anywhere. After *Pur Dicesti* they became most enthusiastic and I could have repeated it, but I just bowed and bowed till they let me go on. I could feel however that I had the audience and I lost all my nervousness. The second group was all French and I had to repeat the Psyche song after a great ovation. The third group went splendidly, especially 'Oh, Cease thy Singing', and in the last group I had to repeat 'Go not Happy Day'.

Denis McSweeney, writing to Lily, painted a more vivid picture:

We have witnessed great demonstrations at the Hippodrome, Symphony Hall in Boston, Sydney and elsewhere, but I can truthfully say that the ovations in both Berlin and Prague were greater. Had the crowd here in Prague been as large as a Hippodrome audience they would have been heard in Paris almost. It was a different kind of enthusiasm. In New York they usually wait for the favourites before they get going; here they started after the first number, sung in Italian, a language which perhaps not a dozen people in the hall understood.

The ovation following the Beethoven Aria in Berlin was simply colossal. I don't think I have ever seen our tenor so deeply touched.

I am happy and very proud and very glad that I got over on time to witness it all, but the joint regret of the Three Musketeers is that you are not here.

The Beethoven aria was from his oratorio, *Christus am Ölberge,* with the Berlin Philharmonic conducted by Bruno Walter. 'I had a great ovation at the close of it,' McCormack wrote to his friend Archbishop Michael Curley. 'This I sang in German. As I said to Teddy it took some nerve to face a German audience and sing for the first time in German an Aria of such importance and that only an Irishman could have done it. Ted agreed.'

He followed this triumph with a recital in Berlin on 2nd May, the first half of which was mainly devoted to Schubert and Wolf and again scored a triumph. *Lieder* or not, the Irish songs did not go amiss. McCormack wrote to Curley on 5th May 1923:

Again the old Irish folksongs carried the day and it was especially amusing to see the broad smiles on the good German faces as I sang 'The Ballynure Ballad' which Your Grace will remember my singing in Baltimore. Would you believe it Your Grace I had to repeat it. Of course the words were printed in German and I am bringing a program to show to you when you come to London. Well everyone was kindness itself and more than enthusiastic, so that I think I may boast that my daring pilgrimage was a success.

Six days later, McCormack gave a notable charity concert on behalf of the devastated regions in Paris at the Théâtre des Champs-Élysées on 8th May in which he sang a programme that included four French composers – Gabriel Fauré, André Messager, Émile Paladilhe and Georges Hué – as well as French songs by César Franck and Padre Martini. Handel was represented by 'Enjoy the Sweet Elysian Groves' from *Alceste,* and McCormack sang Irish songs arranged by Herbert Hughes and one by Charles Villiers

Stanford. The fourth and last part of the concert was given over to modern American and English composers.

The following year in Paris, McCormack participated in the Beethoven Festival at the Théâtre des Champs-Élysées under the direction of Walter Damrosch and the orchestra of the Société des Concerts du Conservatoire. A truly international group of musicians was assembled, including Alfred Cortot, Josef Hofmann and Jascha Heifetz. McCormack again sang the aria from *Christ on the Mount of Olives*, preceded by Beethoven's 'Adelaide' – fortunate the audience who heard him, for he never recorded it.

Having triumphed in Europe, McCormack had still an ambition to fulfil, a nagging one: to be accepted in London again.

CHAPTER FIVE

A Changing World

'London has an indescribable charm,' Lily wrote, 'and nowhere else on earth could the glamour and brilliance of the Royal Opera prior to World War I be equalled.' After the war, the McCormacks continued to return frequently to London, to meet friends and to socialise, but there was no invitation to sing again at the Royal Opera and the Australian debacle made the tenor hesitant to attempt a public recital. From a financial point of view, there was, of course, no reason for him to sing in London and he could have continued his career, dividing his time between the States and the European continent, and taking in Ireland from time to time. But he had had a long association with the London musical scene – it was where he had started after all, and the rejection ran deep. It remained a preoccupation with him. He had thought there was a possibility of making a come back in 1920, and his London agent, Thomas Quinlan, even started making arrangements. However, when the tenor arrived in London, he found that there was ill feeling towards him. He was despondent when he wrote to Wagner on 5th December 1920:

> The London business was a farce. Quinlan is a dreamer, and dreams bad dreams. I knew by the look of him that things were not well and after five minutes talk with him I gave him his £1000 back and cancelled everything. The bitterness against me is very strong and with the present state of things in Ireland it is hopeless... The papers in London were after me all the time but

I only laughed at them and reiterated time and again: I am
American and damn proud of it and I became American because
it is the greatest country in the world.

Two years later, in a letter dated 13th June 1922, he wrote from the Carlton Hotel,
London to Wagner: 'I have given up all idea of singing in England for the present as
there is still a very strong feeling against me.' In 1923, he is more hopeful, writing to
Wagner from St Louis, Missouri, in an undated letter: 'As to London, I will wait
until I get there before making any arrangement as there still may be some feeling in
my regard. I can best gauge that when I arrive on the spot.' But nothing came of
these hopes.

By 1924, it was ten years since McCormack had sung in London and he must have
felt that, with time passing, it was a question of now or never. Amelita Galli-Curci
came to London that year, her legendary reputation preceded by her gramophone
records, and booked the Royal Albert Hall for what the society press described as the
concert of the year. McCormack, playing safe, booked the much smaller Queen's
Hall. It turned out to be an unnecessary precaution. He got, as *The Times* put it, 'an
Albert Hall audience (or as many as could be packed in) in the Queen's Hall'.
However, as soon as his appearance was announced, for 6th October 1924, the tenor
received mail and telegrams threatening disruption of the concert and worse. Although
the memory of what had taken place in Australia must have weighed heavily on him,
he decided to go ahead, come what may. Lily described this concert as the most memorable of any she attended; it must certainly have been the most nerve-wracking.

Henri Deering, the pianist, opened the concert and was, apparently, a model of
composure. Then came the moment when John and Teddy Schneider appeared on
the platform. The packed house simply rose to him and in Lily's words: 'From that
moment the day was John's... John knew he was once again in the hearts of the
British public. We heard nothing more from the writers of the letters and telegrams
and never found out who had instigated the "war of nerves".'

Compton Mackenzie was in the McCormack party and recalled:

> He did me the honour of inviting me to sit between the Countess
> and his daughter in case there was an unpleasant demonstration.
> I had just grown a black beard about that time and looked a bit
> fierce. John himself spent the whole day in church after com-
> municating at early mass, and from the church he came straight
> to Queen's Hall. The place was packed. I sat between the great
> tenor's wife and daughter in the middle of the front row of the
> circle. I can see now John's face, chalk white as he came on to the

179

platform. There was a moment's silence and then the audience broke into mighty applause and cheering. John's face grew whiter, if possible. A silence fell. Then as if from another world he started the aria 'O Sleep' on that high opening note without the ghost of a tremolo in it. [He in fact opened with Scarlatti.] The return to London was a triumph, and not one of the gallant band of anonymous letter writers ventured as loud a hiss as a moulting gander. We had a wonderful supper party that night and a few days later John played over to me the records he had just made of Brahms and Wolf.

The Times, having noted the ovation he received, went on to compliment McCormack on his:

> …very substantial programme. He did not propose the three hackneyed arias with a few ballads, which famous singers often think, no doubt correctly, are good enough for such an audience, but gave a scheme of song in four groups, calculated to show very different sides of his art which, in the years since he was heard here, he has developed considerably. He began with Scarlatti and Handel. The former's 'Caldo sangue' from the cantata *Re di Gerusalemme* is an intensely moving piece of pure melody as he sings it, and his Handel selection in English and Italian, 'O Sleep' from *Semele*, and 'Vanne si superba va', a vigorous aria from *Giustino*, showed two distinct aspects of Handel, as well as the intelligence in interpretation of the singer… His second group was made up of German *lieder*, Schubert, Brahms, and Wolf, his third of Irish folksongs, and his fourth was a miscellaneous selection of things he likes to sing. His study of German song is comparatively recent. If we are not mistaken, he began singing it in public in America only a year or two ago. 'Der Jüngling an der Quelle' (Schubert) had to be repeated, and Wolf's 'Wo'find 'ich Trost', the longest of the group, was splendidly given, though once or twice in the climaxes here one realised that the voice has not quite the inexhaustible quality it used to have. After this group he added as an encore Rachmaninov's 'To the Children' (in English), which he makes extraordinarily appealing through his spontaneous singing. Spontaneity is the very essence of his singing of Irish folksongs. We heard five, and wondered

how many more the audience would get from him. Obviously they could not get enough to satisfy them. In these things the diction is perfect. You hear every word across Queen's Hall, but are not made conscious of the art which produces the result. 'The Next Market Day' (arranged by Herbert Hughes) was spe-

Concert programme London, 24th May 1925. Once McCormack had made his triumphant return to London, only the largest concert hall – the Royal Albert Hall – could accommodate the audiences he drew.

cially captivating to the audience for this reason, but in 'Úna Bán' the singer sings his heart away, which is better still…'

Herman Klein summed up his reception in one word: 'magnificent'. It is ironic that McCormack's triumphant return to London took place the same year that Grove's *Dictionary of Music & Musicians* declared that 'he could no longer be taken altogether seriously as a musician'.

The pattern of his professional life was now set between tours of the States, Britain and Ireland. Summers were spent working on new programmes and relaxing in one

"EVERYTHING KNOWN IN MUSIC"

LYON & HEALY

WABASH AVE. AND JACKSON BLVD.
FACTORIES:
FULLERTON AVE - HEALY STATION C.M. & ST.P.R.R
MAKERS OF
THE LYON & HEALY PIANO
THE LYON & HEALY HARP
THE WASHBURN PIANO
BAND AND STRINGED INSTRUMENTS

TELEPHONE WABASH 7900
CABLE ADDRESS "LYONHEALY" CHICAGO
LIEBER'S AND A.B.C. CODES

EUROPEAN DEPOT
MARKNEUKIRCHEN - SAXONY

REPRESENTATIVES OF
STEINWAY PIANOS AND PIANOLA PIANOS
GENERAL DISTRIBUTORS OF VICTROLAS & RECORDS

CHICAGO, Oct. 21, 1916.

Mr. John Mc Cormack,
% Blackstone Hotel,
Chicago, Illinois.

My dear Mr. Mc Cormack:-

Enclosed is a credit bill for Fifty-five Hundred Dollars for the Nicola Amati violin, a receipt for Five Thousand Dollars on account, and also a receipt for $30.00 for the Hill bow. I hand you also an invoice for the "Wieniavski" Guarnerius on which these various credits apply, leaving a balance which is not payable until about Jan. 1, as suits your convenience.

Our certificate for the Guarnerius will be ready for you next week.

I want to congratulate you as the possessor of the grandest toned violin that I have ever heard.

Thanking you, and with kind regards,

I remain

Yours very truly,

P.S. Is your New York address: c/o Plaza Hotel? If not, let me know and I will change our records next week when I see you.

McCormack, the collector, is congratulated in 1916 by the firm of Lyon & Healy, who sold the tenor a Nicola Amati violin and the 'Wieniavski' Guarnerius. The letter says: 'I want to congratulate you as the possessor the grandest toned violin that I have ever heard.'

McCormack played the piano a little, but he had little skill on the violin. He had wanted to take it up when at Summerhill College, Sligo, but was told it would be a waste of time. Had Summerhill thought otherwise, the world might have gained a violinist but lost a singer. He is supposed to have got himself a mouth organ instead!

The most complete photograph of the McCormack family. John and Lily are standing on the left; with the tenor's sisters, Mary and Aggie in the middle and brother, James, on the extreme right. Andrew and Hannah are seated in the middle. The two McCormack children Gwen and Cyril are in the front on the left with another sister of the tenor's Florrie on the right.

of the several houses he owned or rented in America and the UK. Connecticut had become the location for McCormack family life for many years. Having first rented Pope House in Darien for two years during the war, McCormack then bought his first house, Rocklea, a large, rambling house in a secluded bay in Noroton, a house that Lily remembered with affection:

'Rocklea' had everything John wanted: a bathing beach, a bigger and better dock for the bigger and better boat, a fine tennis court, and a delightful old barn where we had many parties for children and grown-ups. Somewhere along the line John decided that he needed more space for his own work – the big living room seemed to be overrun with children – so he built on a wing; a music room with two guest rooms and baths over it…

John and Teddy would shut themselves in the music room and work for hours on end in blissful privacy, going through the song literature of the German, French, Italian, and Russian masters besides many modern composers. John was very fond of Harry Burleigh and sang one of his songs on nearly every programme. Another favourite was 'Swans' by Walter Kramer.

The mornings the tenor spent in the music room working away with Teddy Schneider left indelible memories for their summer neighbour Laurette Taylor who wrote in an article 'A Big Lump of a Boy' printed in *Town and Country*:

Stretched on the grass beneath the window, I would listen. When he fancied a new song it was an education to hear him and the song get together, the very first time. It was like lovers meeting. He would sing it straight off, and then going painstakingly through it for hours and days to perfect it.

Then there was fishing and yachting. A notable catch was made on board McCormack's boat *Macushla*, when Fritz Kreisler landed a skate. McCormack was not that fond of water, but he took a boy's delight in 'boys' toys' and *Macushla* gave way to *Pal O' Mine*. 'This may have seemed an appropriate name to him, but the boat was no "pal o' mine"!' wrote Lily, 'Cyril was old enough to aid and abet his father in choosing the boat and my protests against their extravagance were in vain. Once more I was called in to help with the decorations and furnishings. I must admit that we had some delightful trips going up to New York on hot days, lunch on deck in the cool breeze, and afternoon tea on the way home.' And there was tennis, with John and maybe Jacques Thibaud against Eugène Ysaÿe and Mischa Elman. As Lily recalled: 'I can see dear old Ysaÿe now his long hair flying as he ran around the court. And after dinner, another evening of heavenly music.'

185

Photograph taken during at party in New York held by the musician Ernest H Schelling, who is standing at the very back with a moustache beneath the taller of the two white ornaments. 'Me' seated on the floor in the centre is the tenor and directly behind him is the soprano Alma Gluck. To her left is the conductor Artur Bodansky and on Gluck's right is the soprano Marcella Sembrich. The pianist, Wilhelm Bachaus, is fourth from Gluck on her left. The critic Richard Aldrich of The New York Times *is the last person in the row on Gluck's right. In the back row third from right is the soprano Maria Jeritza. Also in the back row almost directly beneath the smaller of the two white ornaments is the violinist Efrem Zimbalist (wearing a black bow-tie), who was Alma Gluck's husband. To his right, in the same row, is the violinst Josef Hollman and pianists Alexander Lambert and Artur Schnabel.*

Winters were generally spent in New York with 270 Park Avenue, for many years, being the McCormacks' base from which the tenor would make his concert tours. When artists were together in New York, they would often go to one another's concerts – taking a 'busman's holiday' as Lily put it:

It was during these seasons the most interesting parties took place – when they really let themselves go and behaved like children. To mention a few: Paul Kohanski doing his hat trick; Fritz Kreisler and Toscanini doing coin tricks; Rachmaninov playing jazz; Zimbalist and Ernest Schelling their organ and hairbrush duet; John and Melchior weight lifting; Heifetz in cap and apron cooking bacon and eggs at 4 am; in the earlier days Caruso doing his pencil caricatures. Then when the spirit moved them, we had music which no money could buy. These were some of the unforgettable evenings.

It was also in 1924, after an interval of twelve years that McCormack returned to the Gramophone studios, now located in Hayes, Middlesex. He continued to make most of his records with Victor, while the arrangement between the two companies meant records made in England or America would continue to be marketed by both companies. A preponderance of his art songs was made in England and was intended, seemingly, for the British market. While the Victor recordings were sold in quantity in Britain, the Gramophone recordings did not sell well in America.

McCormack had three recording sessions in September 1924 in Hayes and, had he recorded nothing else, the published records 'from these three sessions would place him apart in terms of his idiomatic fluency and consistency in a selection of music spanning four centuries.

He included *lieder* in all three sessions. These were not, however, his first forays into *lieder*. He had recorded Schubert's 'Ave Maria' in 1913 and 'Ständchen' sung in English translation as 'Serenade' or 'Softly Through the Night is Calling' in 1914. But 1923 was the first time that he recorded *lieder* with the original German texts: Schubert's 'Der Jüngling an der Quelle', which remained unpublished and

The tenor with his father in the back garden of the house he had bought for his parents in Greystones, County Wicklow.

The brothers, John and James McCormack.

188

'Die Liebe hat gelogen', which he recorded again three years later. From this distance, it is difficult to realise the extent to which McCormack was breaking new ground.

Despite his reputation as a singer of ballads, McCormack was something of a pioneer as regards the recording of German *lieder*. With such a wealth of art song on record today, it is hard to believe that the critic Hermann Klein could write in *Gramophone Magazine* in March 1927: 'It is inexplicable to me that so many of Schubert's most beautiful and popular songs should, so far as I am aware, be still unobtainable either in England or the land that gave them birth. Anyhow, only a few have been recorded by a single artist.' McCormack was one. Klein singled out his recording of 'Die Liebe hat gelogen' as having the 'sensations [of a disappointed and betrayed lover] to a nicety.' But added, 'I don't greatly admire his German accent, because it has an American flavour; but it sounds fluent.' Presumably, McCormack had caught something of Teddy Schneider's American accent while learning German from him. McCormack's recordings of Brahms' 'Die Mainacht' and even more so his 'In Waldeseinsamkeit' were singled out by the English critic, the late Desmond Shawe-Taylor observing that they:

> …are sung with a beautiful lightness and smoothness, and with
> an easy phrasing. The interpretation of 'In Waldeseinsamkeit'…
> is notable for the three-fold phrase (like a distant echo) on the
> word 'ferne' and for the final pianissimo rise on the last syllable
> of 'Nachtigall' – one of McCormack's most famous vocal effects
> turned to the most exquisite account. It is hard to think of the
> German tenor who could rival either of these performances.

In these 1924 recording sessions he showed his versatility, putting on disc *lieder* not only by Schubert and Brahms but also Strauss; songs in *stile antico* by Stefano Donaudy (1879–1925), which he loved to sing in concert; adding 'Ridente la calma' by Mozart – his first Mozart recording since 1916 – and Handel's 'Come My Beloved' ('Care Selve') from *Atalanta* which often featured in his programmes.

And he made recordings of Rachmaninov. He knew the composer personally – and was not afraid to disagree with him on tempi, to the point of being adamant, as Lily recounts – and often included his songs in his recitals. The searing parental heartbreak he brings to 'To the Children', on the realisation that the children are children no more, makes this one of his finest recordings of Rachmaninov and a model of its kind.

His friend Fritz Kreisler was on hand to provide a plangent violin obbligato for 'To the Children' and the four other recordings made during this session on 24th

September 1924. In all, the tenor and violinist made twenty-two (published) recordings together between 1914 and 1924.

McCormack included two Irish songs during those September days: Larchet's 'Padraic the Fiddler' and 'I Saw from the Beach' (a traditional Irish tune known as 'Miss Molly') in an arrangement by the folk music collector Herbert Hughes whose work McCormack greatly admired. But it is curious that, although he recorded at this time the most famous of all Irish tunes (excepting only 'Danny Boy'), the traditional 'The Last Rose of Summer' with words by Thomas Moore, it was never released. It is more often sung by soprano, and was used by Friedrick von Flotow (1812–1883) in his opera *Martha* and, at one time, was not infrequently interpolated in the lesson scene in Rossini's *Il Barbiere di Siviglia* and elsewhere. None of that put McCormack off including it in his concerts.

After his London triumph, and having made these records for the Gramophone Company, McCormack returned to the States for his winter tour. The pattern was now well set; the States became the main centre of his career interspersed with frequent visits to Britain and Ireland.

In April 1925, McCormack was back in the Victor studio in Camden, this time recording not into a horn by the old acoustic process but into a microphone. Although electrical amplification had been around for some time, it was only at this point that the recording industry, in need of some development to stir sluggish sales, made the quantum leap forward and adopted the technology – the most important development in the industry since sound recording had been invented. In January 1925, Compton Mackenzie, the editor of *Gramophone Magazine* had informed his readers that:

> We enter our third year at a season when the vitality of the gramophone is popularly supposed to be at its lowest ebb. In spite of that the atmosphere buzzes with whispers of coming excitements. HMV announce a new method of recording electrically.

But, astonishing as it seems now, this new process was greeted with horror and, by November, Mackenzie was bewailing the fact that:

> The exaggeration of sibilants by the new method is abominable, and there is often a harshness which recalls some of the worst excesses of the past. The recording of massed strings is atrocious from an impressionistic standpoint. I don't want to hear symphonies with an American accent. I don't want blue-nosed violins

The tenor with his teacher of old Dr Vincent O'Brien on board ship. O'Brien was McCormack's for his Australian tour of 1913, and made a number of recordings with McCormack and Fritz Kreisler.

and Yankee clarinets. I don't want the piano to sound like a free
lunch counter.

Whatever a free lunch counter may sound like, Mackenzie was not alone in his criticism.
Correspondents to the *Gramophone* were equally negative. Columbia's *Parsifal* excerpts
were 'completely spoilt by the atrocious strident and squeaky tone... even with an ordi-
nary medium toned needle,' complained one writer in horror, 'the din is ear-splitting...'
But this correspondent was restrained compared with the writer who wrote under the
pseudonym 'Indicator' (maybe Mackenzie himself who liked to be provocative):

> It appeared to me to embody potential promise, by reason of its
> greater clarity, breadth and range. But the tone! Zeus! O, ye cir-
> cus round-about organs! O, ye Italian accordions! O, ye screech-
> ing Chinese mothers-in-law!... I thought my old records would
> be worth only the 'pudding price' of 6d each; now it's the
> reverse. Am I a 'realist' or am I kidding myself? Say something
> confrères, or punch me.

The new realism provided by the electrical process had taken listeners by surprise but
it was not only listeners who felt uncomfortable. Among performers, McCormack,
Galli-Curci and Kreisler all regarded the old acoustic process as having been kinder
to their voices and to violin tone. It is true, of course, that records made by the
acoustic process are more mellow in tone by reason of the fact that the upper –
brighter – harmonics did not register as they do on electrically made records.

The new role of the electrical engineer with his twiddly knobs did not find favour
with McCormack either. He had been used to controlling the dynamics of his performance by the simple expedient of moving his head closer or further away from
the recording horn. Now control of the dynamics passed to the engineer.
McCormack was not amused. He took himself into the control room with the comment: 'Who the hell is making this record, you or me?'

McCormack's judicious use of dynamics is well exemplified by his 1916 recording,
in English, of 'The Prize Song' from Wagner's *The Mastersingers* recorded by the old
acoustic process. Walther was a role McCormack harboured an ambition to sing,
although unlike Melba who, unwisely, tried the *Siegfried* Brünnhilde and nearly lost
her voice in the effort, McCormack never sang a Wagner role; although he would occasionally sing arias in recital from operas which require in full performance more vocal
heft than he had by nature.

Any conductor will say that it is an easy matter getting a climax from an orchestra.
It is the lead-up to a climax that presents the challenge, more particularly where there

may be a series of lesser climaxes running in advance. So too with the voice. McCormack eloquently builds up the urgency of this aria, increasing the volume by steps, so that the whole piece is one of development from the gentle beginning until the final, vigorous climax. He demonstrates, as few singers do, that there is little musical value in loud singing in itself; it is the gradations between soft and loud that is musically expressive.

But the new process was, of course, here to stay and the startled response recorded in *Gramophone* soon gave way to enthusiasm. In 1927, McCormack chose to record again some of the songs for which he was most famous: 'I Hear You Calling Me', 'Mother Machree' and 'Kathleen Mavourneen' among them, recordings that gave rise to Max de Schauensee's observation: 'A McCormack Red Seal record was as usual in the average American home, during the second and third decades of the century, as father's slippers by the fire or the family ice-cream freezer.' The voice is in good condition on all these recordings, with no more than a trace of effort in some of the soft high As, which a few years earlier he would have taken without a thought. The electrical process captured the timbre exceptionally well. (Indeed it could argued that modern techniques add so much echo effect and generally egg the pudding to such a degree, that these early electrical recordings provide a more faithful representation of McCormack than many a modern recording does of present day singers.)

What is noteworthy about these 1927 recordings is how much more expansive the vocal personality is, the words ring out with a purpose and meaning hardly equalled by the singer of 1910 or 1911. What makes his personality expansive in these recordings is his *sense of timing*. Not simply the basic underlying rhythm of the song, to which McCormack was always sensitive, but the timing of the communicator: his moving across bar lines to accentuate the verbal meaning of words, the slowing down and the savouring of phrases, the careful emphasis, the gentle portamenti and the caressing of words, all done with the smooth legato line remaining intact.

McCormack represented something of profound and personal importance to Irish emigrants and descendents all over the world through the singing of such songs, the Irish Diaspora being one of the most protracted in history. Although there had been a tradition of emigration since the beginning of the 19th century and indeed much earlier, the main catalyst during Victorian times was the Great Famine of 1845–1847 that decimated rural populations, reducing a population of 8 million by half, according to some estimates – of which a million fled the country in the notorious coffin ships. America was the promised land for most of these emigrants, with others going as far afield as Australia, but all had left a country wretchedly poor. As late as 1873, the Irish artist Alexander Williams (1846–1930), while visiting Achill Island off the west coast, reported seeing families living in dugouts with 'scraws', branches covered with grass sods that served as roofs, at the side of cliffs. McCormack did not represent an idealised

These 'rapid fire' photographs show the tenor in ebullient mood. The extrovert, fun-loving personality he exudes in his maturity contrasts with the early photographs when he comes across as very solemn.

Ireland, rather his art gave recognition to the concept of tears being at the heart of things. It was often said he sang with 'a tear in the voice', with a directness and an immediacy that shunned the bogus and forced sentiment. It was the ineffable sadness of the human condition that he evoked, and the recognition for a people who had nothing else, that it was only through the resources of the human spirit and through personal relationships that life had meaning. So many of his songs contain a wistful yearning for what was or what might have been. 'Though years have stretched their weary lengths between, I hear you calling me'; 'It may be for years and it may be for ever, so why art thou silent, the voice of my heart?'; 'I kiss the dear fingers, so toil worn for me, God bless you and keep you, Mother Machree', his power over language, simple language, direct and forthright, means lines such as these ring in the ears still. In his time, McCormack was part of the consciousness of the Irish people, indeed part of their identity.

There was another side to his singing of Irish ballads, the wry or buoyant humour, self-deprecating sometimes, the shrugging off of adversity, traits expressed in 'Molly Brannigan', 'The Garden where the Praties Grow' and 'Off to Philadelphia' for example. The last song was also recorded by Harry Plunket-Greene who made a hit with it at the Boosey ballad concerts and the contrast between his version and McCormack's is instructive. Plunket-Greene came from a distinguished and affluent

Anglo-Irish family. He was a 'toff' to use a term of the time, and sang the ditty of the emigrant heading off to Philadelphia with condescension and caricature, remaining quite outside the role. McCormack does the opposite, he identifies completely with the plight of the unfortunate emigrant, regrets what he is leaving behind and tells us that there nothing to keep him going for the uncertain future but whimsical hope.

While he was at the height of his powers and celebrity, McCormack maintained a relentless concert schedule. It was unnecessary from a financial point of view. He would still have been an enormously wealthy man without travelling so widely. Even as early as 1916, he was writing to Charles Wagner in a telegram from Los Angeles, dated 21st November:

> …Voice still a little weak. Strongly advise cutting down tour to fifty dates this year. You can arrange, I will sing every Sunday and one week day. Doctor says I simply must be careful or another bout like last may kill goose that lays golden eggs. Warmest greetings. John McCormack.

The strain shows. A telegram dated 21st November 1916 to Charles L Wagner from Los Angeles. McCormack may have thought about reducing his tours to fifty dates, but it was many years before he did so.

Moore Abbey, Monasterevin, County Kildare.

This was a considerable reduction from an earlier suggestion to Wagner that if his manager kept venues close together to reduce travel he would sing 'every other day'. But, he did not come anywhere near his proposed target of fifty concerts. In 1917–18, he sang around eighty-eight concerts, the following year, 1918–19, the number had increased to about ninety and, in 1919–20, he sang around eighty-five. So it went on. The goose was fond of the golden eggs. The financial rewards were huge, but no modern classically trained singer would be likely to attempt these kinds of schedule year on year.

Interior of Moore Abbey.

If McCormack's repertoire expanded during the 1920s, so did his social ambitions. He was now a man of vast wealth. In 1925, he took a fifteen-year lease on Moore Abbey, the home of Lord Drogheda, an enormous Victorian pile in Monasterevin, County Kildare. It must have taken an equally enormous staff to run. During periods spent at Moore Abbey, McCormack could live the life of a grandee, complete with a pheasant shoot that he laid out. Of all the houses they lived in, this was Lily's favourite, not least for its secluded walks, yews and formal gardens. The three children, Cyril, Gwen and Kevin were now at school in England and it was thought it was time for them to get to know 'something of the country in which they were born'. Country pursuits, horse riding and shooting included, now became part of family life.

As much to the point perhaps, County Kildare is in the heart of the Irish thoroughbred industry and the Curragh racecourse is just minutes away from Monasterevin which 'was just right for John'. In fact, it was said that Togher House, the lovely Georgian house in Monasterevin that McCormack took while Moore Abbey was being done up to his requirements, was chosen because it backed onto the railway station from which the Curragh racecourse could be conveniently reached.

True or not, there is no question that McCormack took his horse racing very seriously. Once ensconced in Moore Abbey, he set about pursuing the third of his stated

At the races, Teddy Schneider is on the left next to Lily McCormack.

ambitions, namely to win the English Derby. It was an ambition that remained expensively unfulfilled despite keeping a string of racehorses. The costly venture in farming had taught him nothing about financial restraint. Cyril liked to tell the story that, when his father decided to pack in his horses, they sat down and counted the cost, at the end of which John declared: 'You know Cyril if I had never taken to horses, you would never have had to work.' Lily put it more caustically: 'If John had continued with his horses, we would have been out of the house eating grass with them.' A picturesque exaggeration in both instances, but expenditure on horses somewhat outstripped the horses' ability to win races. A happy exception was Golden Lullaby who won at the Leopardstown races in 1926. There to share the triumph was the world heavyweight boxing champion Gene Tunney, a guest of the tenor. McCormack was something of a celebrity hunter and no doubt the pair revelled in being mobbed wherever they went.

In 1928, the Spanish soprano Lucrezia Bori (1887–1960) was another guest at Moore Abbey. By all accounts a reserved, self-contained person, she seemingly let her hair down when the McCormacks took her off for a visit to Athlone and to Archbishop Curley at his mother's farm where Bori 'spent quite some time playing games with the children in the hayloft' – some memory for the children. Some memory, too, for the congregation at the church in Monasterevin on the occasion when McCormack and Bori both sang there, a combination of voices the likes of which the town had surely never heard before or since.

They both sang in Athlone too, at a Gregorian Mass on 15th August 1928 at which Dr Michael Curley preached the sermon. Admission was by ticket, £1 each, sold by the Marist Brothers and the proceeds were given to charity. The occasion of Bori's visit was the last time McCormack sang in his hometown.

McCormack was a regular communicant, often walking from Moore Abbey to the local church. Should he, for any reason, be late for mass, the parish priest would delay proceedings until his arrival. On one occasion, McCormack was talking to the parish priest in Monasterevin when the rector of the local Anglican church passed by on the other side. Though staunch in his faith, McCormack was an ecumenist in outlook long before it became fashionable to be so. The two clerics did no more than acknowledge each other in the brisk, detached manner of the time. This was not good enough for McCormack, who insisted that the two men introduce themselves. As a result, a friendship grew up between to the two men of the cloth, not a common thing in the Ireland of the 1920s.

If a Derby winner remained outside his reach, McCormack certainly fulfilled his other two ambitions (outside his vocation of singing and early ambition to sing at the Royal Opera, Covent Garden). One was to own a Rolls Royce, which he fulfilled more than a dozen times, albeit not simultaneously.

McCormack had become an art collector early in his career and the third of his ambitions was to own a Franz Hals painting. Lily dated her husband's passion for collecting paintings from 1916 when he bought Corot's *Nymphs Bathing*, but the seeds of collecting and living in the grand manner surely went back to his introduction to Sir John Murray Scott, himself a noted collector and a director of the National Gallery in London. From time to time, *The Times* reported on the tenor's acquisitions. On 19th January 1917, it was announced that he had bought from Sir Audley Neeld, Rembrandt's *The Burgomaster* 'for a large sum for his home in the United States'. From Christie's, it was reported on 21st March 1921, that he had paid the sum of 5,000 guineas for Romney's *Clavering Children*. His ambition to own a Franz Hals was fulfilled when he acquired *Man* from the Zamoisky Collection in the Blue Palace, Warsaw, for which he paid a reputed price of $90,000.

On New Year's Day 1925, in New York, McCormack made his first radio broadcast on the pioneering medium, with Lucrezia Bori. It was a widely publicised event. His easy manner, in addition to his singing, attracted a large audience and he continued to broadcast regularly up to 1942. In all, he probably made several hundred radio appearances. About twenty broadcasts are known to exist still, although others

McCormack receives an enthusiastic review during his Japanese tour.

The Japan Times & Mail

TOKYO, WEDNESDAY, MAY 5, 1926

McCormack Scores Wonderful Success In Second Concert

Makes His Audience Smile and Sigh by Turn and Weaves Spells of Fairyland

Last evening in the Imperial Theater John McCormack treated the large audience to a galaxy of ballads and arias. His voice, always sweet and warm, last night partook of the finer qualities of liquid expression and soulful interpretation.

The very first number showed Tokyo the superb mastery of his lyric voice and demonstrated what has been his secret of success and popularity—that indefinable Irish brogue, though only slight, yet what a charm it lends to the song, what a feeling it stirs within the heart.

Complete Repertoire

McCormack took his audience back to the stirring times when knights and ladies and chivalrous cavaliers were a common sight on every

may turn up. Their quality is variable and, until the mid-1930s, generally poor. Nevertheless, they are of interest as historical documents, containing, in several instances, music McCormack never otherwise recorded – including Mendelssohn's 'On Wings of Song' (in 1927 and again in 1933) and 'Alma mia' from Handel's opera *Floridante* (broadcast in 1934).

Following the advice of his friend, Fritz Kreisler, who had made a lucrative tour in the Orient, McCormack did the same in 1926. His tour included five concerts at the Imperial Theatre in Tokyo. Once the tour was arranged, *The Japan Times* announced his imminent arrival, describing him as the singer of 'Mother O' Mine'.

McCormack's proposed concert programmes were also announced in advance. They make interesting reading as an indication of how much wider McCormack's repertoire was, particularly in early music, than his discography or reputation would suggest; and once again it refutes the mistaken belief that McCormack ever confined himself to familiar ballads. In the first concert, Handel's 'O sleep why dost thou leave me?', one of his favourite concert arias and one he did record, was followed by a rare piece by Leonardo Vinci (*c.*1690–1732) 'Sentire! Il petto accendere' from his opera *Artaserse*. His second concert opened with the aria 'Gioite al canto mio' from one of the very earliest of all operas *Euridice*, by Jacopo Peri (1561–1633), followed by Handel's 'Enjoy the sweet Elysian Groves' from *Alceste*; and his fourth and fifth con-

200

certs featured respectively Mozart's 'Per pietà non ricercate' and from Handel's little known opera *Giustino* 'Vanne si superba va'. The third concert opened with the recitative and aria from Beethoven's oratorio, *Christ on the Mount of Olives*, then continued with Schubert and Wolf. Nineteenth and twentieth-century music was represented throughout, along with a collection of Irish songs.

The programming worked. 'McCormack scores wonderful success in second concert', ran the heading in *The Japan Times*, noting that: 'His voice, always sweet and warm, last night partook of the finer qualities of liquid expression and soulful interpretation... The very first number showed Tokyo the superb lyric mastery of his voice.' The paper also spoke of his 'complete repertoire', which first 'took his audience back to the stirring times... in old 18th century oratorios and operas' – and quickly homed in on the Irish ballads 'the most interesting part of his repertoire'. In May 1926, the paper then reported the impression made on one of McCormack's admirers:

> When he first came in, I sort of expected him to act as if he were 'the World's Greatest Tenor'. He did not. He just went and leaned up against the piano and, if he'd been in his own parlor at home, he couldn't have been more simple. It seemed as though we were all one big family, and he was just talking to us, quietly, with his head a little on one side, and his eyes closed, telling us fairy tales as they came into his mind, making us smile and sigh by turns, weaving spells about us, and sometimes wringing our hearts by the pathos of his tones... Once he got settled by the piano he'd not shift his position at all, hardly; and you'd find yourself listening to that quiet soothing voice, that just came with no apparent effort, and seemed to be talking confidentially to each individual in the theatre.

In conjunction with the Tokyo concerts, The Ginza Gramophone Store took advertisements in the *The Japan Times*, first of all to announce that a consignment of McCormack gramophone records were on their way to the store. And, secondly, to announce what they were when they arrived. They were all Irish or Irish-style ballads, every one of them, including 'God Save Ireland' and 'A Nation Once Again', released on doubled-sided Odeons. Whatever and wherever McCormack might sing in the world, he was identified with Irish song, and for a sizeable proportion of his admirers, it was to the exclusion of well-nigh all else. (Yet when, some years later, HMV offered a subscription series (limited to 500 sets) of Hugo Wolf recordings, in which McCormack had participated, sales were initially sluggish in the UK, but more than 100 sets were quickly taken up by Japanese music lovers.)

Advertisement on a bus, beneath McCormack's name in smaller print, too faint to be seen in the photograph, is the name of his film Song O' My Heart. *Evidently his name carried more weight than that of the film. Its poor showing at the box office may have been on account of the absence of love scenes.*

In 1929, when he was forty-five years old, McCormack signed up with Fox to make a full-length feature 'talkie' film. Unlike any of its immediate predecessors, the film had a continuous soundtrack, and McCormack was the first singer ever to make such a film. It had no title to begin with, nor indeed a proper script as we would understand the term but, by a process of working on the thing as it went along, the film *Song O' My Heart* emerged.

Attempts to harness sound with moving film of famous singers had been made since at least the beginning of the century. Opera singers made 'audible shorts', brief films or episodes to which cylinders and discs were played at appropriate moments. Another method was to assemble a cast of actors to mime, as synchronously as possible, to a record not of their own making. A group of French actors did this in 1911 to the Victor recording of the Sextet from *Lucia di Lammermoor* featuring Caruso, Marcella Sembrich, Antonio Scotti *et al* recorded in 1908.

In the mid-1920s, Warners developed the Vitaphone system that made synchronous sound, through disc recording, a practical, commercial proposition. The method would be quickly superseded by sound-on-film systems of which Movietone, used by Fox, was one. However, Vitaphone was a huge step forward in film technology, as a result of which a host of Metropolitan stars, Giovanni Martinelli, Beniamino Gigli (later an enthusiastic film star), Ernestine Schumann-Heink and many others appeared on Warners Vitaphone 'shorts' singing their hearts out. It is surprising, however, how ingrained the idea had been that film was essentially a silent medium albeit with live musical accompaniment, and that, in that state, it lacked for nothing. Charlie Chaplin was not alone in asserting that movies with sound would never catch on. To a generation brought up on the silent screen, the idea of adding sound seemed like an intrusion, and they thought nothing of sitting and watching the silent antics not merely of actors, but of singers too, even of Caruso.

On the set of Song O' My Heart. *Teddy Schneider at the piano, McCormack leaning against it on the left with Maureen O'Sullivan.*

Al Jolson changed all that. He both spoke and sang in *The Jazz Singer* (1927) and when it was first screened in New York, the film created a sensation. A whole generation of silent film stars who could not make the transition to sound were swept away, not always with a good grace. The Hungarian actress, Lya De Putti left Hollywood with the words: 'Talkies are the bunk. They will pass and there will be much disappointment over them... America will realise its folly and the producers

McCormack with Frank Borzage, the director of Song O' My Heart.

will be clamouring for us to come back.' They did not; instead they looked for performers who would not only look good on screen but sound good too.

To Winfield Sheehan, vice-president of production at Fox, McCormack seemed the ideal candidate for a 'talkie' on account of his widespread fame, boyish charm, and not least because he spoke English with a pleasant, recognisable brogue and not with the heavy accent of a foreigner. To which might be added that the tenor was still young enough, in his mid-forties, although he was overweight. He did, however, diet in advance of filming and although not exactly slim, at least he looks the same for the duration of the film. The same could not have been said of Mario Lanza when he appeared in *Because You're Mine* in 1952. An undisciplined comfort eater, Lanza had a propensity to put on weight very easily. As a result, in one sequence a slim Lanza enters a barrack room and, in the next shot inside the room, he suddenly appears fat.

A contract was signed in May 1929 in New York in which it was agreed that McCormack would receive a fee of $500,000, 20 per cent of which was payable on signing. Production was to begin about November when the tenor would receive the balance of his fee in 10 per cent instalments during the eight weeks of filming. Frank Borzage, a Hollywood heavyweight, with such acclaimed films behind him as

Seventh Heaven (1927) and *Street Angel* (1928), both starring Janet Gaynor and Charles Farrell, was chosen as director. The contract required McCormack to sing between six and eight songs in English of his own choice with the number to be determined by the producer; and three more songs that should be in French, Italian or German, again at the singer's discretion. In the event, the standard version of the film contains twelve songs, if 'The Magpie's Nest', a snatch of just a few bars, is included.

ALICE JOYCE
AND
TOMMY CLIFFORD

MAUREEN O'SULLIVAN

The film was made in standard 35mm format and also in what was known as Fox Grandeur, a 70 mm wide screen format, which had the added advantage of a sound-track 7 mm wide as against the standard 2 mm used. Early press releases announced that this soundtrack actually enhanced McCormack's voice. However, the film was never released in Fox Grandeur and it is not known if a copy survives. Typically for the time, for non-English speaking markets the dialogue was removed and a continuous musical score added along with intertitles.

At the time of the contract, the fact that no story or script existed for the projected film would not have been considered of any great importance: the singing would be the thing, along with a few sentimental scenes. The storyline of *Song O' My Heart,* like many of the films of the time, is simple and uncomplicated. In this instance, small-town boy, Sean O'Carolan, becomes famous because of his golden voice, a story not far removed from McCormack's own. Alice Joyce played the role of Mary O'Brien, Sean's childhood sweetheart. Mary is a widow by the time she meets up with Sean again, and has a large family to support, the most notable of them being daughter Eileen, played by Maureen O'Sullivan (1911–1998). O'Sullivan was born in Boyle, County Roscommon and had always dreamt of a film career. It came to her earlier than she expected. Frank Borzage was in Dublin while he was selecting locations in and around Moore Abbey for filming, when he happened to come across the svelte and beautiful eighteen-year-old O'Sullivan and immediately employed her. This was the start of her film career, remembered now primarily, perhaps, for her scantily clad appearances as Jane in a number of Tarzan films. *Song O' My Heart* had none of that kind of thing, indeed its charm lies, at least in part, in its innocence.

Although McCormack had made it quite plain to Borzage from the start that he was not going to try to be a screen lover, no doubt remembering with less than affection his awkward attempts at being a stage lover in opera, Borzage almost certainly had other ideas and had probably presumed that he might work some love scenes into the film during shooting. Borzage's previous films, after all, embodied in the words of one film reviewer, Paul Taylor, an 'uncompromising romanticism' and *Street Angel* had centred around an *amour fou*. But McCormack was having none of it. 'Finding a story to suit John,' Lily wrote,' was difficult. He hated love scenes, and if one was written into the scenario, he'd have it cut out. So the script was changed from day

McCormack exchanges a few words with J M Kerrigan and Farrell McDonald, who are seen in close-up below.

to day. Frank Borzage was the soul of patience and did a masterly job of directing with one hand, and keeping the peace between John and the script writers with the other. As long as there were no loves scenes there was peace…'

There was another singer in the cast, the bass Andrés De Segurola, a distinguished veteran of the Metropolitan opera, who played the part of Guido. He had already partnered Gloria Swanson in *The Love of Sunya* (1927) and went on to make *One Night of Love* (1934) with Grace Moore, among other films. The opportunity to provide an element of musical contrast by having a bass as well as a tenor was not taken, as de Segurola was given only a speaking part.

In August 1929, Borzage and his Hollywood crew journeyed to Moore Abbey (which McCormack was leasing at the time) to film there. The area around the property consists of flat, rolling countryside, pleasant rather than spectacular, but Borzage liked what he found and had a small cabin built on the River Barrow that winds through the grounds of the house. Using this cabin, one memorable episode in the film has McCormack singing 'A Fairy Story by the Fire' surrounded by a group of small children. Another is when he sings 'Just for Today' in a tiny, local church. The practice, that was soon to become common, of pre-recording music with the singer then filmed miming to the record was not used in *Song O' My Heart*. So these and other scenes from the film are examples of early 'field' recording.

Scattered through the film are songs that McCormack had already made popular on disc. 'The Rose of Tralee', which he had recently come across, he sings twice. 'I Feel You Near Me' was especially written for the film by Joseph McCarthy and James Hanley, while the film's theme song, 'A Pair of Blue Eyes', was written in-house by

The quintessential McCormack in white tie and tails, his eyes closed and his head thrown back in intense concentration.

William Kernell, a Fox member of staff. The ditty 'Kitty my Love, will you Marry me', a folksong from the Herbert Hughes collection, is a good example of the rhythmic impetus McCormack could bring to a song. He never made a studio recording of it. McCormack sings 'The Magpie's Nest', which lasts just a few seconds, to settle an argument between two characters, Peter and Rafferty, as to whether he really has the 'ny-ah' in his voice. This little sequence is a period piece of Hollywood's idea of Irish banter.

In the story, Sean gives up his promising singing career in order to look after Eileen and her brood of children, but not before we hear him singing in concert in

"MOORE ABBEY"

FIFTH DAY'S SALE

FRIDAY, 19th FEBRUARY, 1937

Commencing at 12 noon.

THE PRINCIPAL BEDROOMS—(Continued).

THE ALCOVE BEDROOM.

THE PRINCIPAL BATHROOM.

THE GARDEN BEDROOM.

THE LAWN BEDROOM.

THE GRAND STAIRCASE AND LANDING.

THE DOMESTIC OFFICES.

THE BUTLER'S PANTRY.

THE KITCHEN (including: Batterie de Cuisine, Coppers, etc.).

THE DAIRY.

THE COURTYARD
(Garden Furniture, Tools and Implements).

PONY, TRAP AND CART, HARNESS.

PONY, MILCH COW, ETC.

Moore Abbey, Monasterevin, County Kildare, auction notices.

New York. All credit is due to Frank Borzage for providing this sequence of four songs, filmed at the Philharmonic Auditorium in Los Angeles. It brings us closer to McCormack as a recitalist than any other visual record. In white tie and tails, the tenor, holding his little black prompt book, and with Teddy Schneider at the piano, sings one song after another, without any inter-cutting to star-crossed lovers or the like that could so easily have spoiled the sequence. Neither before nor since has such a sequence been included in a feature film.

The little black prompt book had its origins in an early concert in Dublin when his memory failed him while singing 'Once Again'. Thereafter, he had the words of each song written out in a loose-leaf black book, more as a psychological prop than anything else as he did not refer to the words in it. And, in time, the book probably became a physical prop, something to clasp with his hands. In the film, the characteristic manner – the head is thrown back, the closed eyes, the fervent expression, the overwhelming sense of commitment to every line that draws the listener in – may be taken as typical of the singer, a pose familiar to countless concert goers.

Song O' My Heart had its premiere on 11th March 1930, at the 44th Street Theatre on Broadway, a venue more prestigious than a conventional movie theatre. The enthusiastic critical response it initially received was not matched at the box office. Perhaps the very sequences that McCormack had been determined to avoid, against the best efforts of Borzage and the scriptwriters, were the ones that might have made the film more popular. At any rate, Fox did not take up its option for a second feature film with the tenor.

By the time McCormack appeared in a feature again, this time making a guest appearance as himself, he was eight years older and cut a decidedly portly figure.

Wings of the Morning (1937) with Henry Fonda, Annabella, Lelie Banks and Irene Vanbrugh, was the first British film to be shot in Technicolor. In it, McCormack sings three songs, but this time the focus is as much on the intercut picturesque and romantic scenes as on the singer and the voice, in any case, was nothing like as fresh as in *Song O' My Heart.*

Having fun in the pool at San Patrizio.

Film making, even if it did not lead to a film career, gave McCormack a taste for Hollywood and for entertaining, on a lavish scale, the big names of the day. But, when he decided to relinquish the lease on Moore Abbey, which still had three years to run, and move to California, he appears to have done so with an element of bitterness. On 1st June 1937, he wrote from California to his friend Monsignor Arthur Ryan:

> It was a grievous wrench to give up Moore Abbey, but I could not feel that I could be of the slightest use to my own people there. In fact I thought at times that they were inclined to resent my intrusion, and the Tailtean Games episode, which I told you of, was the straw that broke the camel's back. I have a feeling that every new Government adopts instinctively as its motto 'Timeo Danaos et dona ferentes' ['I fear Greeks even when they bear gifts'].

Entertaining at San Patrizio. John and Lily McCormack are in the centre, on the left are Frohlie Mulhern and Frank Crummit and on the right the Abbey Actor F J McCormick (Peter Judge). The Abbey Players were entertained at San Patrizio during a tour of the States.

The Tailteann Games, a revival of ancient Irish games, were held in 1924, 1928 and 1932. What slight or perceived slight that should have continued to rankle over so many years, is not known. It is possible that he aired the idea that he would like some sort of official government post by which to make a contribution to Irish artistic affairs and he may have been rebuffed. He did express such a desire a few years later, after he had retired. But clearly it was not only towards Athlone that the tenor had ambiguous feelings.

He bought a cottage in Hollywood, California on 163 acres, tore it down and built his own home, San Patrizio. 'The *Song O' My Heart* money,' wrote Lily, 'a not inconsiderable sum, remained in Hollywood, with a lot more following it… 'San Patrizio' was not a large house but it had an enormous music room acoustically perfect. This was the first, and last, house that John built. During the seven years we owned it we considered it our real home.'

By the end of the 1920s, McCormack had established himself in all the media open to him: opera, the solo recital, the recording industry, radio, which was the most pervasive medium of his time, and film. Through the 1920s, particularly in the second half of the decade, his voice aged perceptibly and was no longer the consistent instrument it had once been, and he knew it. Quite why McCormack's voice

A galaxy of champions being entertained by the McCormacks at San Patrizio in 1932. From left to right: Lily McCormack; Cecily Nelson (friend of the family); the US tennis champion in 1912–13 Maurice McLoughlin; Gwen McCormack; Michael Beary (Aga Khan jockey); the author Edgar Wallace; Ellsworth Vines also a US tennis champion (1931–32), and John McCormack. This, incidentally, was the last photograph taken of Edgar Wallace.

declined so relatively early, while still in his forties, is not clear. Conventional wisdom suggests that a well-produced voice will go on indefinitely, and few voices have been produced with less apparent strain or forcing that McCormack's. His voice appeared to survive the near fatal streptococcal throat infection he had in 1922, but the illness may have weakened his constitution. Even after his illness, his concert schedule, for many years, was both relentless and gruelling. It has been suggested that, by singing only in recital in a repertoire of congenial keys, his voice lost the elasticity that exercising in and for opera would have continued to provide. Less

John with Cyril and Gwen taken in San Francisco in 1912. He represented an ideal of Irish-American manhood.

obviously, garrulity too has been suggested as possibly having affected the vocal chords. Voice specialist, Dr Martin Cooper, in *Great Singers on Great Singing* goes so far as to assert: 'The speaking voice of the singer is seldom trained and often misused and inefficient... Misuse and abuse of the speaking voice may negatively influence and affect, if not destroy, the singing voice.' Certainly McCormack was a great talker and a smoker to boot. He enjoyed high living and he looks uncomfortably heavy and prematurely old in photographs from the 1930s. So, though conventional wisdom may hold otherwise, if other parts of the body may age prematurely and without any apparent abuse as they appear to do, why should the vocal chords be any different? There is always the question of genes and luck.

Yet, in spite of all this, in 1930, McCormack was to make a recording that required the stamina of youth and is one which stands as one of the greatest examples of oratorio singing on record. The top has not the freedom it would have had just a few years earlier, but, a year or two later, and the record could not have been made at all. It is the recitative and aria from Beethoven's *Christ on the Mount of Olives* recorded with the RCA Victor Orchestra conducted by Nathaniel Shilkret. Remarkably, it was not published in his lifetime. The recitative he recorded in both German and English, the aria in English only. It is difficult to think of another singer who could bring such fervour and drama to this piece yet make all the telling effects exclusively through musical means. The enunciation of the recitative is a joy in its clarity of form. In the aria, for all the drama it contains, the line is never smudged; the intonation is exemplary and his use of language as powerfully delivered as in any recording he made. And with no sense of his vocal resources being tried, he builds up the aria with religious fervour to the final repeated outbursts of 'Lord, deliver me', the voice finally and slowly and gently ebbing away on the extended 'me'. It is a finely judged performance.

With the death of Enrico Caruso in 1921, McCormack's celebrity status in the States was virtually unrivalled and it remained so through the 1920s. Women had always made up the larger part of his audience. For many, he represented an ideal of Irish-American manhood, with exceptional looks on top of the beguiling voice. His status was reflected in the honours he received. Early in 1917, he was made Doctor of Literature at Holy Cross College, Massachusetts; he became a Freeman of the City of Dublin in 1923; a Doctor of Music at National University of Ireland in 1927; and,

in 1933, he received the Laetare Medal from the University of Notre Dame. The Roman Catholic Church recognised his merits with several honours, beginning in 1913 when he was made a Commander of the Holy Sepulchre and several more followed; culminating in 1928 in the honour of which he was most proud: that of being raised to the Papal Peerage by Pope Pius XI in recognition of his unstinting work on behalf of charities. The honour was the greater for being made hereditary. As of writing, the title is held by the tenor's grandson, also John, Count McCormack.

In 1932, the 31st International Eucharistic Congress was held in Dublin. The pope was represented by his Legate, Cardinal Lauri. Not since the days of the great orator Daniel O'Connell, with his vast public meetings at the beginning of the 19th century, had such crowds assembled. The congress concluded on Sunday 26th June, with

McCormack as a bearer of the canopy at the Eucharistic Congress of 1932.

a Pontifical High Mass held in the Phoenix Park on the outskirts of the city with a congregation estimated at 1 million. The *Irish Press* reported the arrival of the faithful in purple prose:

> Night had hardly come and gone when along the Park roads the sound of footsteps rang and shadows passed among the trees. Full daylight showed these early groups resting here and there; men and women both. Movement far away towards the Ashtown gate told that with the dawn the cars were coming too. As the light strengthened the individual footsteps sounding through the morning became first the heavier beat of many groups, and then by eight o'clock the steady tramp of an army. On, on, on never broken, never stopping, it came; from the south, from the north, from the east, from the west – men and women, boys and girls, without ceasing, without pause.
>
> There were the voices of the world among them, and all our own inflection – the sharp music of the north, the soft accents of the south, the lilt of the western speech.
>
> There were many old men and women dust covered, weary walking that long, hard road through the centre of the Park. Many thousands were resting on the grass edges, unending human banks, between which the human torrent flowed…

H V Morton, writing for the London *Daily Herald* reported that:

> It is a crowd so vast that it lies over a square mile of parkland, hiding every blade of grass. A carpet a mile square, picked out with a pale pattern that is hundreds of thousands of human faces, brightened with countless specks of red and blue which are the clothes of women.

Selection of photographs from the Eucharistic Congress of 1932.

How great is it? No one can say… All I can say about it is that no crowd quite like it has ever been seen in our time. So great is the awed silence of this incredible host as it watches the white throne, that you can hear a bird singing among the trees and the

wild cries of gulls that have come from the coast and wheel above
the altar.

Religion and politics are rarely far apart in Ireland, and the *Dundalk Examiner*
reminded its readers that the faithful had:

> …assembled in a land which has held the Faith in spite of cen-
> turies of persecution, famine and dispersal. There were Irish there
> who had travelled thousands of miles to assist at the greatest of
> Eucharistic Congresses. They or their fathers had gone from a
> land made poor for the sake of the very doctrine which they so
> tirelessly returned to affirm.

Standing at the high altar, McCormack, resplendent in his papal uniform, had the
largest live audience of his career. He sang the 'Panis Angelicus' from César Franck's
Mass in A. Appropriately, the musical director for the congress was his teacher of old,
Dr Vincent O'Brien. In anticipation of the broadcast of the congress, sales of radios
(or wirelesses as they were better known at the time) sold briskly in the Irish Free
State. McCormack's singing was to have been heard in the Vatican, with the pope
waiting to receive it, had the transmission not broken down. A recording, however,
was made and is extant as is separate newsreel footage. More or less successful
attempts have been made to put both together. Transmission the other way round
was more successful, with the pope's message being heard across the Phoenix Park,
Reuter's New Agency reporting that: 'A few minutes later the Pope was assured by
telephone from Dublin, that his words had been heard perfectly.'

CHAPTER SIX

The Final Years

It was the American soprano, Lillian Nordica (1857–1914), who said: 'A prima donna dies no less than three times: first go her looks, that is death number one; then her voice, that is number two; and finally the death she shares with the others.' Nordica need not have confined her bleak comment to prima donnas. Singing tends to be the prerogative of youth and few singers sound as well after fifty, to take a significant date, as they did before; and those Italian tenors who maintain the same effervescent repertoire of their younger days tend to do so with declining élan and virility.

In the 1930s, McCormack was still an international celebrity and household name although the voice was declining. It was a measure of the artist that he could still make magic with both words and music and, although the soaring melodic contours of his youth were behind him, some of his most persuasive records were yet to come.

He chose his repertoire wisely, it not only suited his contracted vocal range, but revealed the added dimension of maturity. Twenty-seven years separate his 1907 Odeon recording of 'Terence's Farewell to Kathleen' from the Victor version of 1934. It is a more worldly-wise Terence we get the second time round. If it is the youthful timbre and spirit that immediately capture the attention in the first, it is Terence's plight in the second. When he sings 'But I'm sure that you'll never deceive me' in 1907, Terence gives the impression that he believes it, even providing a little triumphant emphasis to the word 'never'. In the second recording, Terence would like to convince himself that Kathleen will come back to him, but cannot do so. How plaintive, in the Victor version, are the lines: 'And when you come back to me,

The tenor photographed with Colonel Fritz Brasé of the Free State Army Band.

Kathleen,/ None the better shall I be off then–/ You'll be speaking such beautiful English,/ Oh, I won't ['That I shan't' in the Odeon version] know my Kathleen again.' Terence's world is falling apart and we are made to feel it. In 'The Garden where the Praties Grow' (1930), a whimsical song which McCormack sings with both brio and charm – never rushing it, although there is a temptation to do so. In the lines 'O the parents they consented and we're blessed with children three,/ Two boys just like their mother and a girl's the image of me', the chuckle he provides on 'the girl's the image of me', has the emphasis of a man who has known fatherhood and can look back upon it. And, in 1940, almost at the end of his recording career, he makes of 'The Bard of Armagh' (arranged by Herbert Hughes), a broken, solitary figure of almost heartbreaking intensity. In simple, direct lines, as at the end of this song, in the plainest of lines McCormack can evoke the strongest feelings of loss: 'By the side of my Kathleen, my young wife, oh place me;/ Then forget Phelim Brady, the Bard of Armagh.'

McCormack had a special affinity with Hugo Wolf, responding to the questioning, searching nature of Wolf's work, its religious allusions and to Wolf's organic fusion of music and language. And it was in the 1930s that McCormack produced some of his best work in *lieder*. The Wolf Society was formed by HMV in 1931 for the purpose of producing limited editions to be sold by subscription; in all, six volumes of Wolf's songs were published. Elena Gerhardt (1883–1961) was the first singer approached and, over a period of years, some fourteen singers recorded for the project. McCormack introduced to America some of the orchestral settings that Wolf had made for his songs. For the Wolf Society, he is accompanied by Teddy Schneider. His 1932 recording of 'Ganymed' is regarded as one of the high points of his recording career. Desmond Shawe-Taylor wrote of it:

> He does supreme justice to one of the greatest of all German songs. It is somewhat mysterious that McCormack seldom (if ever) sang in public a song of which his interpretation is so memorable, indeed haunting, as to seem definitive. This is one of those rare performances which may properly be called inspired. A gentle pulsation enters the voice at the new access of emotion on the words 'Du kühlst den brennenden/ Durst meines Busens/ Lieblicher Morgenwind!' a wondering assent at 'Ich komm! Ich komme!', a rapturous excitement at the phrase 'Mir! Mir!/ In euerm Schoße Auwärts!', while the long final phrase floats upward and out of sight, from the oft-repeated D to the high F sharp, in a manner of which this singer alone knew the secret.

In contrast to 'Ganymed', McCormack recorded Wolf's 'Schlafendes Jesuskind', a poetic meditation on a painting by Francesco Albani, no less than three times in 1925, 1930 and 1936. If the voice is inevitably older sounding in the last recording, it is also the one in which the singer is perhaps most deeply committed; and his recording of 'Herr, was trägt der Boden hier' (1935) has the powerful stamp of a singer who not only understands mortality but anticipates it. In a different vein altogether, yet still the work of maturity, is the unforced, spontaneous charm he brings to 'Auch kleine Dinge', also recorded in 1935, an existential savouring of the passing moment

McCormack's own favourite photograph.

– the observation that 'Auch kleine Dinge können uns entzücken' ('even small things can delight us') – is relished and pondered upon in a way that tends to escape youth. These recordings, made in the autumn of his career, are remarkable in showing that the singer, even as his voice declined, did not cease to develop experientally as well as idiomatically; the freshness of his art, the urgency in his communication, remaining to the end.

The breadth of McCormack's repertoire was immeasurably larger than that of almost all his contemporaries; as a singer he could move from popular ditties of the day, to Irish ballads, to Rachmaninov and modern-English art songs and *lieder* and, at the same time, embrace 18th and 19th-century opera – a remarkable achievement. But times were changing and what was once regarded as popular was becoming less so.

If he expanded his repertoire in the 1920s in one direction with German *lieder*, he expanded it in another with American popular music. He anticipated Paul Whiteman and his band's big hit of 1923 'Three O'Clock', by recording it in 1922, complete with the sound of London's most prominent clock, Big Ben, an exotic touch for a song originating from New Orleans! His last acoustic recording session with Victor in New York in 1924 yielded up Irving Berlin's 'All Alone' from *Primrose* and the title tune from Oscar Hammerstein's *Rose Marie*. He recorded 'Sonny Boy' in 1928, the same year as Al Jolson, and recorded another Jolson favourite 'Little Pal' the following year. It was not that McCormack could not sing such music, sing it he could of course, but his vocal identity was nourished by, and belonged in, a different world, the world of the Victorian and Edwardian ballad and salon music and of grand opera. It was indicative of how the musical world was diverging. The time was approaching when a difference would be made between the so-called 'serious' singer on the one hand and a 'popular' singer on the other. In McCormack's youth, there was no such distinction, for the reason that everyone sang in much the same way or tried to, whether it was in opera or around the piano in the parlour at home.

Now a schism was at hand. Al Jolson on one occasion in 1932 dramatically pushed a microphone away from him with the comment: 'It's a sad day when Jolie needs a mike to sing into.' It was an anachronistic gesture even as he made it. The microphone may at first have been seen as nothing more than a useful tool for providing volume to voices that needed it, but it quickly became something quite different: an integral component of a new way of singing. The stars of the opera had been remote figures on the stage, made more remote by the masks they adopted and the roles they played. In the words of Michael Scott in *The Record of Singing*:

> Rubini, Mario and Jean de Reszke were greatly admired, but
> their reputations had not extended far outside the opera house
> or beyond the society that patronised it. Indeed, Jean de Reszke

rarely appeared in concert, and then only in excerpts from opera; throughout his entire career he never sang a song.

Audiences were changing and McCormack, as himself, on the concert platform had offered a much more accessible and personal form of communication, which was more in keeping with changing times. This process of greater accessibility, more intimate contact, did not end with McCormack, but he was the last full-voiced singer to carry the process forward. The emerging microphone style of vocalism would bring an altogether greater sense of familiarity and informality to singing, to the point that the old full-voiced style, however intimate the personality behind it, would appear old fashioned, even strange, to the rising generation. When Laurence Tibbett was being presented as a movie star in the 1930s, the promoters thought better of announcing him as a celebrity of the Metropolitan Opera. Opera no longer had the cachet it once had.

Bing Crosby recognised very clearly the transformation that was taking place in public taste as regards the new microphone style of singing versus the old. In his 1983 autobiography, *Going My Way*, he wrote:

> I think – and I'm confident that my assumption is correct – that every man who… listens to one of my records or who hears me on the radio believes firmly that he sings as well as I do, especially when he's in the bathroom shower. It's no trick for him to believe this, because I have none of the mannerisms of a trained singer and I have very little voice. If I've achieved any success as a warbler it's because I've managed to keep the kind of naturalness in my style, my phrasing and my mannerisms which any Joe Doakes possesses.
>
> They feel no kinship for a wonderful register and an elaborate range. They realize that he's achieved something they can never hope to achieve. But it's my hunch that most men feel that if they had gotten the opportunity I've had, they could have done just as well.

Inevitably with new vocal styles come new music; and the Afro-American and American popular music exclusively associated with the microphone voice would eventually sweep away the Victorian and Edwardian ballad from public consciousness. Opera, too, was no longer the contemporary art form it had been before the First World War, with little written since then entering the standard repertory.

McCormack found himself engaged on radio, exchanging small talk and pleasantries with Rudy Vallee and Bing Crosby, quite a different thing from sharing a programme with such Metropolitan Opera favourites as the Spanish soprano, Lucrezia Bori. There is, however, every indication that he enjoyed such encounters, and was ever receptive to good singing of whatever kind, wherever he heard it. He was an admirer of Bing Crosby.

In two consecutive years, he had first a joyous event, followed by one of personal loss. In 1933, his daughter Gwendoline married Edward Pyke at the Brompton Oratory in London. Her father, now well and truly a count, was eager to appear at the wedding in his papal uniform. Gwen pointed out that the day was hers rather than his and he was not going to steal the limelight. Instead he sang 'Panis Angelicus' and, according to Lily, '…he *did* steal the limelight… in spite of the radiant bride and handsome groom, two tiny pages in white satin, and eight pretty bridesmaids in pale blue with velvet caps, carrying sheafs of pink flowers.' Lily should have been radiant too. Outside her hotel had been left a cream and black Rolls Royce, a present from John.

The following spring, in 1934, the McCormacks left for a South African tour, for once without Denis McSweeney who had been ill – he died later the same year.

McCormack and Lily on walkabout in Capetown, during his tour of South Africa in 1934.

A final bow. McCormack gave his last concert in England before his retirement at the Royal Albert Hall, London on 27th November 1938. Gerald Moore is on the left.

McCormack felt his loss keenly, having depended upon 'Mac' for so long. He had been with the singer since the beginning of his concert career and his sole manager since the early 1920s, '…after that,' wrote Lily, 'things were never the same. John grew restless and moody and couldn't settle down to anything, even life in "San Patrizio"'.

Lily said that he had intended to retire at fifty. In fact, at one time, he had thought of retiring very much earlier, writing to Charles Wagner: 'You know how I have always talked of retiring at forty.' But McCormack would not be the first performer to find that, as the years go by, the intended date of retirement tends to be postponed. However, after McSweeney's death, with the tenor's brother Jim now acting as manager, he decided to do just one more concert tour of the States. This took him up to 16th March 1937, when he gave his final concert at Buffalo, departing, *The New York Times* noted with 'a gay wave of his hand and a soft good-bye, drowned in thunderous applause'. A tour of Britain and Ireland followed in 1938 concluding with a concert on 27th November at the Royal Albert Hall in London, with Gerald Moore as his accompanist. *The Times* reported:

> As many people as the Albert Hall will hold gathered yesterday to hear Mr [sic] John McCormack sing for the last time in public.

FAMOUS TENOR'S FAREWELL

McCORMACK AT THE ALBERT HALL

RETIREMENT AT 54

By RICHARD CAPELL

Many thousands were present—there was, in fact, hardly a vacant seat to be seen—at John McCormack's farewell concert yesterday at the Albert Hall. It was the kind of audience that already applauds at the beginning of a song, if the tune is recognised; and by four o'clock people were shouting for their favourite pieces.

Mr. McCormack is only 54, but if his admirers regret his early retirement he has, at least, spared them the sad spectacle, usual at these Albert Hall farewells, of a crumbling ruin. Time, indeed, has only begun to touch his art. True, he can no longer sustain a classical melody as he did 30 years ago, when he

COUNT JOHN McCORMACK singing at the Albert Hall yesterday.

Newsclipping of final performances.

'The clear, sweet singer' – how precisely Longfellow's adjectives describe him! To the sweetness of tone, which, for all its taint of nasal quality, remains beautiful because it is unforced, and to the remarkable clarity of his words, that carried almost unfailingly through the vast space, Mr McCormack adds a rare command of legato. His phrasing yesterday was always lovely, even when his rhythm was not impeccable. And so he carried his great audience with him unfailingly through a programme of quiet, elegiac songs – almost it was an anthology of 'Songs of Farewell' – that few singers could have saved from monotony. There were representatives of the various kinds of music that have supplied his repertory during his thirty year career – excepting perhaps too strenuous operatic arias – an air by Handel, two songs by Hugo Wolf, Franck's 'Panis Angelicus', some ballads, and, what the audience evidently most wanted, a selection of those traditional songs of Ireland which he sings with an inimitable charm.

229

It would be idle to pretend that his voice retains its freshness and power; but it is still beautiful to hear because it has always been well produced and his skill in using it remains as sure as ever.

There was a song, 'The Old House', by General Sir Frederick O'Connor that was written especially for McCormack's farewell tour, the last lines of which run:

Lone is the house now and lonely the moorland
The children are scattered, the old folk are gone,
Why stand I hear like a ghost and shadow,
'Tis time I was moving, 'tis time I passed on.

BOSTON SUNDAY POST — YOUR WORLD -- FEBRUARY 27, 1944

McCormack's Mass Appeal Was Greater Than Crooners'

Changing times. The Boston Sunday Post, *27th February 1944. That a newspaper should choose to make a comparison between McCormack and Frank Sinatra indicates how much had changed in the world of music since the tenor had started out. McCormack is represented in the role of Tonio from* The Daughter of the Regiment. *Sinatra is shown, appropriately, holding a microphone.*

It was too much for Lily. When he sang it at his farewell at the Theatre Royal in Dublin, Cyril had to escort his mother out of the auditorium.

In 1944, *The Boston Sunday Post* wrote a profile on McCormack and then went to pose the question: which singer was most likely to succeed him? The answer that the newspaper came up with was Frank Sinatra. It was a revealing choice, showing how far the world of music had changed since McCormack's young days. It is interesting to note too that Bing Crosby, who cut his first disc in 1929, had his first million seller ten years later, the year after McCormack's retirement. When Gerald Moore asked the tenor why he had chosen to retire from performing in the States, when vocally he was still in a position to go on, McCormack, always the man to give a direct answer, replied: 'I lost my audience.'

It was between the decline of opera as a contemporary art form on the one hand and the rise of the genre of the popular microphone singer on the other, that McCormack had been an icon and manifestation of an age: the most celebrated concert platform singer of his time.

McCormack made a few more radio broadcasts in the US after his farewell concert and, for a period, he may have been uncertain as to what do next. Teddy Schneider decided that this was the time for him to retire too and he bought a small house in Arizona. 'It meant a lot to him to have his own little home,' Lily wrote, 'and he felt that he'd done enough travelling for a while. I can never forget how sad John was when we left Teddy standing at the station. I am glad that neither of them knew they would not be seeing each other again.'

The vacuum that follows retirement is hardly ever easy, and is probably hardest of all for a performer who has been fêted and adored wherever he has gone, and who had spent the greater part of his life in constant travel. Eventually, John and Lily decided to sell up in the States, disposing of San Patrizio and moving to London, to be closer to the family. McCormack had spent a fortune – several indeed – but was still a wealthy man. Lily's caution had seen to that.

McCormack took a place in Berkeley Square, London W1, a notably prestigious address, with a view to starting up as a singing teacher. But the idea was short lived. Great singers rarely make great teachers, the skills of performance are instinctive rather than prescriptive, and McCormack had little aptitude for describing 'how he did it'. Besides, he had no patience for teaching. He could be brusque with aspiring youngsters and he had shown an aversion to giving auditions, regarding them as an imposition. To one pompous young man, who asked having done his party piece: 'What do you think of my execution?' McCormack could not resist replying: 'I am in entire agreement.' To another he had used the ultimate put-down, remarking when the unfortunate singer had finished: 'Didn't Teddy play great?', leaving the tyro to draw his own conclusions.

231

One of the last photographs of the tenor, taken at his home Glena, in Booterstown, County Dublin, accompanying the young tenor, Christopher Lynch.

McCormack fishing on the River Slaney, Ireland.

Being unwell in the summer of 1939, he decided to have a fishing trip. He rented Shean Lodge on the salmon-rich River Owenmore, which runs through the wild, desolate landscape of County Mayo in the west of Ireland. Always fond of company, he wrote, on 9th June, from Shean Lodge to his old friend Monsignor Arthur Ryan imploring him to join himself and Lily, Cyril and Aunty for the tenor's birthday on 14th June: 'We came down here to this wonderful spot to catch or rather seek the elusive Salmo Ferox but alas and alack, no rain no fish. Did you ever hear of anyone cursing fine weather in Ireland; well, here's one.' The term *Salmo ferox* may have appealed to McCormack for its ring, i.e. ferox – 'spirited'. It is a freshwater trout found in Ireland but not in the Owenmore, which has runs of Atlantic salmon and sea trout.

Patience was not among the singer's most prominent virtues, and word has it that he responded to fruitless efforts on the river bank not merely by casting his line into the water, but rod and reel with it. His gillie, Frank McManamon, dutifully retrieved the tackle as needed. Despite the hot, dry weather on 17th June and subsequent days,

Wartime advertisement saying that John McCormack and the Irish comedian Jimmy O'Dea (1899–1965) would present, time and about, a weekly series Irish Half-Hour *aimed 'particularly for the Irish men and Irish women serving in the Forces'.*

John McCormack and Jimmy O'Dea in

'IRISH HALF-HOUR'

The great Irish singer and the great Irish comedian will take turn and turn about in a new weekly series designed particularly for the Irishmen and Irishwomen serving in the Forces. Count John McCormack will be the star of the first 'Irish Half-Hour' to be broadcast on Saturday night. Jimmy O'Dea will carry on the good work the following Saturday, and after that this happy 'Box and Cox' arrangement will continue until further notice.

as the records for the lodge show, he caught a 10lb salmon and five sea trout averaging 2lbs each. Arthur Ryan did not make it down in time for McCormack's fifty-fifth birthday, but arrived on 9th July and appended a note of his own to another letter from John: 'I went thank God, and on my first day on the river, John's gillie tied a fly for me, and on my first cast I caught a lovely wee trout!'

Eric Craigie, a member of the Shean fishing syndicate, recalled visiting the lodge at ten in the morning:

> …when John was singing like a nightingale in his bath (he loved the soft river water). Back to a lunch of seagull's eggs and oysters; I had two fish and my brother, one, and John was so pleased that he gave us the best vintage champagne in return for our keeping the larder stocked with salmon and black-headed gull's eggs which I collected each day from Corrib. Hearing the Count singing in the bath was something to remember.

To guests who visited the lodge, McCormack is said to have sung, appropriately enough, 'Moonlight in Mayo'. And those who made up the congregation in the church in the tiny village of Ballycroy must have been astonished on one occasion to find the man often billed as 'the world's greatest tenor', serving the Mass as an altar boy and participating in the choir. Outside in the churchyard, seeing that the moon was still visible, he suddenly gave an impromptu rendering of 'The Moon Behind the Hill'. And when entertaining the parish priest, Father Anthony Timlin, for dinner at the lodge, he sang a Paternoster by Palestrina. He had rented the lodge for two months but, in the event, he stayed only six weeks. The impression is of a man not content in retirement.

With the outbreak of the Second World War, McCormack responded eagerly, offering his services to the Red Cross. He was back in his element. With Gerald Moore as his accompanist and with the baritone Robert Irwin and contralto Sara Buckley as assisting artists, he toured the English provinces and sang to the British troops. It was ironic that McCormack's last and most loyal audiences were to be in England during the Second World War, a country where he had been unable to sing during the First. Between the autumn of 1939 and May 1940, McCormack gave close on forty concerts. Lily worried that the strain of touring might be too much for him, but to be working again raised his spirits. He was still in touch with Charles Wagner and wrote to him from his house in Woodend, South Ascot, on 11th September 1940 in high spirits:

> I am back in harness singing for the Red Cross and broadcasting to the army and navy and the Heroic and unforgettable air men. What men, and what fighters against unspeakable odds. The people here are wonderful… Lily joins in kind regards. You should see Gwen's Patricia [the tenor's first grandchild]. She is lovely and the image of *me*! Now no remarks!

> Your old friend

> John McCormack.

Recording sessions continued with Gerald Moore as the accompanist until 1942. He could still work magic over material that did not make too great a demand on his declining vocal resources. It was his power over language, rather than any extended vocal line, the nuances he could bring to small pieces such as 'She Moved Thro' the Fair' and 'Off to Philadelphia', both recorded in 1941, that make these recordings memorable and even minor works of art. He was less successful with Mozart's 'Ave verum corpus' recorded during his last session of all on 10th August 1942. He had left it too late to record the hymn, the extended legato line is inevitably absent and his intonation had become uncertain. Maybe he believed that some of the old vigour would yet return because there was no indication that he realised this was to be his last recording session. His final broadcast, for the BBC, took place earlier in the year,

Towards the end. A BBC broadcast where the tenor does not look well.

on 2nd January, when he was interviewed and sang in Dame Irene Vanbrugh's house in London along with Maggie Teyte, Eileen Joyce, Herbert Dannison and Gerald Moore.

With teaching abandoned and now in poor health, McCormack lived for eighteen months in the Shelbourne Hotel in Dublin. He set his sights on buying another large house near Dublin, which would have required a sizeable staff to run. Lily persuaded him otherwise and they moved to Glena in Booterstown, County Dublin, a more modest house facing the sea, where it was hoped his health might improve. He was subject to constant colds and he again developed a streptococcal infection. Each illness seemed to reduce his vigour further.

He had expressed an interest in some kind of government post promoting the arts but no invitations came his way. There was even talk of him standing as a presidential candidate in 1945. Nothing came of that either and his health would not have stood it in any case. It would also have involved the question of changing his nationality as he was still an American citizen. By oversight or otherwise, the McCormacks were not invited to the presidential inaugural reception held in Dublin Castle in June for

Sean T Ó Ceallaigh. For a man who had sung for kings and queens and who had been befriended by American presidents, this must have been a bitter moment.

Yet for all that Lily paints a picture of quiet peace in those last days: 'My memories of the twilight of John's life are necessarily simple ones. He was never more contented, and I have often wondered if he didn't realise that the race was nearly run. We had lots of fun together in small ways…' There was the joy of playing with his grandchildren Patricia and Carol Ann, Cyril's first born. But to his friend Canon Sydney

Glena in Booterstown, County Dublin, the tenor's last home.

MacEwan he admitted another side to his thoughts: 'Sydney, I'm sixty and I hate it!' He still entertained when he could. The Irish pianist, Charles Lynch, was one of the last to visit him and remembered him singing, or maybe half speaking, a few bars of Wagner, of all things. Singing of any kind became impossible with the development of emphysema that reduced even his speaking voice to a whisper and curtailed his mobility, although not his humour. Near the end, he turned to one of his nurses and said gently: 'Do y'know if Christ ever sang, I am sure it was with a tenor voice!'

There were now only the records left, and occasional broadcasts of previously recorded material from Radio Éireann and the BBC, which he would listen to wistfully and perhaps with an element almost of disbelief at all he had achieved.

On Tuesday 11th September 1945, five years to the day when he had written to Charles Wagner in high spirits telling him he was 'back in harness', he caught a chill. At first it did not seem serious but it turned into pneumonia and as he began to sink into unconsciousness it was apparent that he would not recover. Lily and Cyril were present when the end came on the evening of 16th September at 11.25 pm. He was sixty-one.

The following day, Lily received members of State and Church who called with their condolences, including President Sean T Ó Ceallaigh, Taoiseach Eamon de Valera, the Papal Nuncio and the Archbishop of Dublin. Telegrams came from all over the world, from Teddy Schneider and Gerald Moore, and from Dorothy Caruso, widow of the tenor, who wrote from New Jersey: 'No one in this world understands how you feel tonight better than I do. I wish I could be with you. My heart yearns for you.' Caruso's daughter Gloria Caruso Murray also sent a telegram.

At his home, Glena, *The Independent* noted: 'The world famous tenor lay in state in the colourful full-dress uniform of a Papal Count. On his breast were Papal decorations while his sword lay by his side on the bier.'

Dr Vincent O'Brien wrote a tribute in *The Independent*: 'Ireland today laments the departure of one of her most distinguished sons, one who sang the joys, the sorrows, and the hopes of the Motherland in the ear of a listening world. "If the pulse of the patriot soldier or lover has throbbed at his lay", it will be their duty to remember John in the way he himself would have dearly wished – by a prayer to the Giver of all good gifts that he may find that Pax Dei, which he himself so often brought to troubled hearts the world over with the gentle message of his song. "Go sleep with the sunshine of fame on thy slumber."'

On 17th September, his remains were removed to the local Church of the Assumption. The funeral, held the following day, was 'one of the largest in Dublin for many years and was attended by the president, the Taoiseach, members of the diplomatic corps, the Church, the Lord Mayor of Dublin and many from the performing arts. The *Irish Press* recorded that: 'The austerity of the Requiem was softened by the light September sun and the profusion of red and white flowers of the wreaths, which transformed a corner of the little Church of the Assumption at Booterstown into a dazzling garden.' Crowds lined the route from the church to Dean's Grange Cemetery. At the graveside, the Palestrina Choir, conducted by the Rev. A Griffith CC, sang *Benedictus*. A headstone, with a carved cross at the top and a wreath below framing a bronze bust of the tenor, marks the grave.

Lily McCormack lived on for nearly twenty-six years after John's death. She moved back to New York to be among the many friends that they had made there. It was on a return visit to Dublin in 1970, to visit her son Cyril and her grandchildren, that she suffered a stroke. She died a year later on 26th April 1971 and is buried in the family plot in Dean's Grange Cemetery.

It is to be wondered if McCormack could ever have achieved what he did or retained his pre-eminence for so long without Lily's constant support and love. What she felt for John comes across clearly in her book *I Hear you Calling Me*. The love was mutual. 'Thank God for Lily,' John exclaimed in one letter to Charles Wagner. 'But then I was born lucky.' He was.

Max de Schauensee was a critic who heard most of McCormack's contemporaries and the Irish tenor himself many times. In a pen portrait of the singer published in *Hi-Fidelity Magazine* in February 1957, he recalled the impression McCormack had made on him:

> When I think of the word 'singer' stripped of any extraneous dramatic connotations and in its purest sense, I see John McCormack standing on the concert platform – his head thrown back, his eyes closed, in his hands the little black book he always carried, open but never glanced at, as he wove a spell over his completely hushed listeners. John McCormack was truly a singer for the people; he was also a singer's singer.

There is no one left now who can remember John McCormack. We are left with the testimony of his genius through his recordings, around 800 in all. They remain as evidence of his musicianship, the versatility and consistency of his art, no matter what he sang. He had many of the greatest virtues that one associates with singing: a voice of great purity and beauty; immaculate diction; the ability to shape the vocal line with the same delicacy as a stringed instrument. He was a consummate vocal technician. But above the beauty of the voice and the security of his technique, what is apparent, even when the voice was no longer young and vigorous, is that McCormack remained always a vividly communicative artist; among the most compelling vocal personalities of the 20th century. He has not been replaced.

Glossary of Terms

bel canto literally 'beautiful song' but more often used to describe a particular kind of singing, associated with the 18th and early-19th century and with composers such as Rossini, Donizetti and Bellini.

coloratura singing that involves rapid scale passages, octave leaps, trills, runs and all manner of florid and bravura vocal display. Once all singers, whatever their vocal range, could produce fioritura or coloratura. It was said that the great French bass, Pol Plancon (1854–1914), could produce coloratura to compete with any prima donna and his party piece was to do exactly that, singing in falsetto. Coloratura has more or less fallen into disuse except among some high sopranos who specialise in the art and, less frequently, tenors.

contralto lowest female voice. The term is also used for low voices of boys and the adult male falsetto voice or counter-tenor, also referred to as alto.

legato from *legare* meaning to tie. The ability to move from one note to the next with perfect smoothness, so producing a legato line, as opposed to staccato in which the notes are all sounded separately.

mask used by singing teachers. Auto-suggestion forms an essential element in the way the voice is produced. Producing the voice 'in the mask' is suggestive of projecting the voice towards the front of the face, in particular towards the forehead, around the nose and resonating cavities: the sinuses behind the cheekbones.

mezza voce literally 'half-voice' in reference to volume of sound. Surprising as it may seem, to sing *mezza voce*, halfway between singing softly and loudly, is one of the most difficult things to accomplish, particularly in the middle range of the voice. McCormack had one of the most secure vocal techniques and could sing *mezza voce* with ease. Caruso, remembered for his powerful top notes and wonderful climaxes was also noted for the beauty of his *mezza voce* singing. You hear less *mezza voce* singing today, for the simple reason that singers are competing against louder orchestral playing.

obbligato literally 'essential', but the word is perhaps better understood as 'important'. Reference to an important solo passage or passages for an instrument in a composition written primarily for another instrument or for the voice.

pianissimo to sing or play very softly.

portamento (plural **portamenti**) from *portare* to carry, the technique by which a voice or instrument moves between notes, especially notes widely separated, without a break. In other words gliding from one note to another.

primo tenore literally 'first tenor'.

répétiteur musician employed to coach singers in learning scores. Typically, an operatic *répétiteur* will emulate the orchestra with a piano reduction of the score, so that the singer or chorus can learn their parts in relation to what the orchestra may be doing.

stile antico, literally 'the antique style'. The composer Stefano Donaudy (1879–1925) was much given to composing in the style of the 18th century, requiring singing with a long-drawn legato line, exactly the kind of thing in which McCormack excelled. He often sang Donaudy's compositions in concert and recorded a number of them.

tenore robusto literally 'robust tenor voice', the sort of voice suitable for the heavier operatic roles. *Tenore robusto* is the same vocal classification as the German *helden-tenor*. The Italian term *tenore di forza* is similar, meaning the ability to sing at full voice with force, 'raising the roof'. It should not be thought that the *tenore robusto*, by nature, is not capable of refined and accurate singing, although too often big voiced tenors degenerate into bellowing. The creator of Verdi's Othello, Francesco Tamagno (1850–1905), who is reckoned to have had one of the most powerful tenor voices of all time, could sing and declaim with a vocal control and accuracy that is astounding; as his records, although made at the end of his life, clearly demonstrate.

tonic sol-fa, system of musical notation without notes or staves and used to assist in the sight reading of music, especially by choirs. The system was invented in the 19th century by John Curwen (1816–1880).

Bibliography

The best bibliographic reference on John McCormack, like many other subjects, is the internet. As of writing, Paul W Worth has an extensive bibliography of books and articles on his website (www.jump.net/~pwworth/biodex.html) on the tenor and it is regularly updated. There is no need to repeat it here. The printed material I have consulted and quoted from is listed among the acknowledgements at the front of the book. The main books and articles relating to the tenor's life and career are:

Dolan, Peter, 'John McCormack, Mastersinger: A Short Account of His American Career' *Sword of Light* (Spring 1974).

Foxall, Raymond, *John McCormack* (New York: Alba House, 1963).

French, Florence, 'First Authentic Story of John McCormack's Life and Career' *Musical Leader* (14th June 1917).

Key, Pierre V R (transcribed by), *John McCormack: His Own Life Story* (Boston: Small, Maynard & Co., 1918). Vienna House 1973 edition, edited and with an introduction by John Scarry.

Ledbetter, Gordon T, *The Great Irish Tenor* (London: G Duckworth, 1977).

McCormack, Lily, *I Hear You Calling Me* (Milwaukee: Bruce, 1949).

O'Brien, Gearoid, 'John McCormack and Athlone' The Old Athlone Society (1992).

Smith, Gus, *John McCormack – a Voice to Remember* (Dublin: Madison, 1995).

Strong, L A G, *John McCormack – The Story of a Singer* (New York: MacMillan, 1941).

Ward, John, 'McCormack on Brighton Pier' *The Record Collector* XXXVII (1992)

Index

247